Adam Mickiewicz

THE SONNETS
INCLUDING THE EROTIC SONNETS,
THE CRIMEAN SONNETS, AND
UNCOLLECTED SONNETS

GLAGOSLAV PUBLICATIONS

THE SONNETS

INCLUDING THE EROTIC SONNETS,
THE CRIMEAN SONNETS, AND UNCOLLECTED SONNETS

by Adam Mickiewicz

Translated from the Polish and introduced by
Charles S. Kraszewski

This book has been published with the support
of the ©POLAND Translation Program

Publishers
Maxim Hodak & Max Mendor

Introduction © 2018, Charles S. Kraszewski

© 2018, Glagoslav Publications

www.glagoslav.com

ISBN: 978-1-911414-90-2

A catalogue record for this book is available from the British Library.

This book is in copyright. No part of this publication may be reproduced, stored in a retrieval system or transmitted in any form or by any means without the prior permission in writing of the publisher, nor be otherwise circulated in any form of binding or cover other than that in which it is published without a similar condition, including this condition, being imposed on the subsequent purchaser.

Adam Mickiewicz

THE SONNETS
INCLUDING THE EROTIC SONNETS,
THE CRIMEAN SONNETS, AND
UNCOLLECTED SONNETS

Translated from the Polish
and introduced by Charles S. Kraszewski

GLAGOSLAV PUBLICATIONS

Contents

INTRODUCTION: A POET FOR EVERYONE,
A POET FOR NONE. ADAM MICKIEWICZ AND HIS SONNETS. . . 7

THE EROTIC SONNETS 35

THE CRIMEAN SONNETS 81

UNCOLLECTED SONNETS 119

THE POET'S CLARIFICATIONS 136

TRANSLATOR'S NOTES 144

BIBLIOGRAPHY 178

ABOUT THE AUTHOR 180

ABOUT THE TRANSLATOR 181

Adam Mickiewicz

1798 – 1855

A Poet for Everyone, a Poet for None

Adam Mickiewicz and his *Sonnets*

Adam Mickiewicz, the man who was to become the father of Polish Romanticism and his country's foremost poet, was born on Christmas Eve, 1798, in Zaosie, Lithuania. This is important. Not that he was born on Christmas Eve — which can lead to exaggerated comparisons, nor that he was to become the national bard (a fate Shakespeare, perhaps, still shakes his head at in irritation) — that is a title, a definition, a circumscription, however glorious. It is important, rather, that he was born, that he was a human being, which is something, as in the case of Shakespeare, that we often forget.

And so Mickiewicz was no more than 28 when he wrote the following lines:

> Z tobą tylko szczęśliwy, z tobą, moja droga!
> Bogu chwała, że taką zdarzył mi kochankę,
> I kochance, że uczy chwalić Pana Boga.
>
> [Only with you [am I] happy, my dear! / Praise be to God, Who has bestowed such a lover upon me, / and praised be my lover, who teaches me to praise the Lord God.]

We should bear this in mind as we read through the *Erotic Sonnets*. Mickiewicz was still a young man, a handsome young man, with a healthy erotic appetite,* and all of the idealistic élan with which, not only the Romantic period (for which it is often caricatured), but

---

*   "With great stubbornness and in various ways the hagiographers have striven to extricate themselves from it [*Mickiewicz's sexual appetite, something far from the elevated ideal of the unhappy lover*], now by pooh-poohing the matter of Mickiewicz's conquests (during the course of which he even succeeded in seducing his future mother-in-law, which is, when all is said and done, a rather rare accomplishment), now dispensing fatherly moral exhortations to youth itself, is marked. There is nothing particularly insincere about the lines from sonnet I:

> Ledwieś piosnkę zaczęła, jużem łzy uronił:
> Twój głos wnikał do serca i za duszę chwytał;
> Zdało się, że ją anioł po imieniu witał,
> I w zegar niebios chwilę zbawienia zadzwonił.
>
> [You'd barely begun your song, and already I was weeping; / your voice penetrated my heart and grasped hold of my soul; / It seemed that an angel was greeting her by name, / and the clocktower of the heavens sounded the moment of salvation.]

And the giddy silliness with which "Good Night" comes to an end, besides being giddy and silly, has a vibrancy about it that points to lived experience:

> Dobranoc! obróć jeszcze raz na mnie oczęta,
> Pozwól lica. — Dobranoc! — Chcesz na sługi klasnąć?
> Daj mi pierś ucałować. — Dobranoc! zapięta.
>
> — Dobranoc! już uciekłaś i drzwi chcesz zatrzasnąć.
> Dobranoc ci przez klamkę — niestety! zamknięta!
> Powtarzając: dobranoc! nie dałbym ci zasnąć.
>
> [Good night! turn your little eyes toward me, one more time, / let me kiss you upon the cheek. — Good night! — Do you want to clap for your servants? / Let me kiss your breast. — Good night! all buttoned up. // — Good night! Now you've escaped, and you'd like to slam the door. / [I'll say] Good night to you through the keyhole — Alas! locked! / Repeating "Good night," I'd not let you fall asleep.]

The problem is, by the time that Mickiewicz published the sonnets in 1826, he already had a sizeable body of "serious" poetry behind him,

---

him, now spreading wide their hands." Jan Walc, *Architekt Arki* (Chotomów: Verba, 1991), p. 73.

from the groundbreaking *Ballady i romanse* [Ballads and Romances, 1822], which had the same effect on the development of Polish literature as Wordsworth and Coleridge's *Lyrical Ballads* had for English, through the first two published sections of *Dziady* [Forefathers' Eve, parts II and IV, 1823], which inaugurate the genre of monumental drama in Poland (and, consequently, Europe), and are rightly compared to the work of both Dante and Goethe.

 This is the Adam Mickiewicz best known to Poles: the *wieszcz narodowy*, or National Bard, who nourished the souls of his countrymen with elevated, patriotic verse during the dark night of the national tragedy of the Partitions. It is often the hero, the patron saint, the demi-god, that Poles look for in their poets, and when they appear in the guise of normal human beings, the reaction is rarely positive. This seems to have been the case since the very start of Mickiewicz's career, judging by the verse with which the *Erotic* cycle comes to an end:

> Nuciłem o miłostkach w rówienników tłumie;
> Jedni mię pochwalili, a drudzy szeptali:
> „Ten wieszcz kocha się tylko, męczy się i żali,
> Nic innego nie czuje lub śpiewać nie umie.
>
> „W dojrzalsze wchodząc lata, przy starszym rozumie,
> Czemu serce płomykiem tak dziecinnym pali?
> Czyliż mu na to wieszczy głos bogowie dali,
> Aby o sobie tylko w każdej nucił dumie?"
>
> Wielkomyślna przestroga! — wnet z górnymi duchy
> Alcejski chwytam bardon, i strojem Ursyna
> Ledwiem zaczął przegrywać, aż cała drużyna
>
> Rozpierzchła się unosząc zadziwione słuchy;
> Zrywam struny i w Letę ciskam bardon głuchy.
> Taki wieszcz jaki słuchacz.
>
> [I sang of love's adventures in a crowd of my contemporaries; / some of them praised me, while others whispered: / "That bard only loves, suffers, and laments; / he feels nothing else,

or doesn't know how to sing. // Now that he's entering upon more mature years, with an older reason [[more sense, a settled mind]], / why does his heart burn with such a childish little flame? / Is it for this reason that the gods give him a bardic voice, / so that he'd only croon about himself in each poem?" // A magnanimous warning! — so, right away, like the more elevated spirits, / I grasped the lyre of Alcaeus, but in Ursyn's robes [[or: in Ursyn's style]] / I'd hardly begun playing, when the whole troop of them // scattered, astonished at what they heard. / So I tore away the strings and tossed the deaf and dumb lyre into the Lethe. / The listener gets the bard he deserves.
es.]

You don't mind Goethe and Dante, in other words, but you have no patience for Petrarch? You don't mind the poet as the unacknowledged, or even acknowledged, legislator of the nation, but you won't allow that legislator to be a poet?

That the same determined devotion to keep Mickiewicz from stepping off his nationalistic pedestal is still around in our own day and age, consider what Jan Walc says about the *Crimean Sonnets* in his *Architect of the Ark* — one of the most entertaining bio-critical essays on the Polish poet. The *Sonnets*, as we know, were published in Moscow, with the imprimatur of the Tsarist censors. And yet:

> They allowed the little volume to be printed and — as so often happens — they understood nothing about it nor did they learn anything. After all, the while that the Crimean Tatars were first being taken in hand, Mickiewicz warned them that *the spring remains*. What is even stranger is that the Polish receptors of the poems, supposedly trained in sifting out political allusions from their readings (and this includes learned historians of literature), for a century and a half now stubbornly hold to the conviction that the *Crimean Sonnets* are chiefly dedicated to the description of nature.*

---

*   Walc, p. 77.

Is it not possible that this is because there *are no* political allusions in them, and that they actually *are* "chiefly dedicated to the description of nature?" Well, poetry, like the Bible, can be interpreted in many ways; even in conflicting ones. This is why we speak of *valid and invalid* interpretations, not right and wrong ones. The only criterion is that the interpretation should be provable on the basis of the text itself, without having anything foreign being read into it. So, the words of the harem fountain in Bakchysarai, alluded to by Walc, can be seen as a general comment upon the inexorably fleet passage of all that is human, in contrast to the staying power of grander Nature, and as a prophetic warning to enslaving Russia; a prophetic consolation to Poland enslaved.

The power of great poetry, such as the *Crimean Sonnets*, lies in its ability to speak authentically to more than one narrow constituency. For one quick example of this, consider the various ways in which critics have spoken of the narrator's "glance into the abyss" from the top of Chufut-Kale. For Michał Kuziak, it is a Schilleresque expression of Romantic sublimity, the "expression of content out of the reach of mimetic aesthetics, and in this way exceeding the aesthetics of the beautiful:"

> Sublimity, being a sign of mystery, of limitlessness, discloses also the limitations of the human person, the existence of a dimension that goes beyond the cognitive possibilities of reason (constituting on the other hand the object of experience), and, as such, ineffable, impossible to express in speech.[*]

Alina Witkowska, similarly to Kuziak, but perhaps more in line with nineteenth century thought (Shelley might sigh about the yearnings of a moth for a star, but still, deep inside, he fostered the hope that the moth *just might* reach it after all) speaks of the insatiability of the romantic narrator — somewhat along the lines of Goethe's eternally striving optimist, Faust:

> The pilgrim reveals his presence as a romantic philosopher of nature, above all, in the sonnet entitled "Path on the Chasm

---

[*] Michał Kuziak, *Inny Mickiewicz* (Gdańsk: Słowo/Obraz terytoria, 2013), p. 57.

in Chufut-Kale." He is the opposite of his reasonable guide, the Mirza, who advises him not to try and search out the unplumbed abysses of being. The pilgrim is characterised by cognitive maximalism, and boldness, and an unrestrained desire to penetrate the mysteries of being — all characteristics of the philosophising poets of the Novalis type.*

Finally, Walc (a traditional Pole, despite all the seeming iconoclasm of his archly entertaining *Architect of the Ark*), interprets the poem along the run-of-the-mill lines of patriotic poetics:

> *Mirza, and I looked!* The pilgrim does not turn his glance aside. This is a figure, in miniature, of Mickiewicz's experiences in Russia — that Russia, which ought to terrify the poet with its immensity, presenting him with an understanding of his own smallness and weakness. It is in that direction that his Crimean guide — the *mirza*, the defeated Asian — wishes to direct him. But the Pilgrim catches sight of the spring, which remained, even if others can't see it, and can't understand its significance. The pilgrim knows, and sees, more than they — it was not in vain, his boast concerning his falcon-like eye, his hawk-like sight; the perspective of history is open to him.**

Both critics compare the European narrator to his local guide. It seems to us that both Witkowska, with her opposition of the "reasonable," that is to say cautious, *mirza*, to the bold narrator, and Walc, with his "defeated Asian," are exaggerating a bit, in order to pump up the heroism of that Polish narrator. After all, the *mirza* is the one who bravely forces his horse to soar over the abyss between two cliffs — the Polish rider will only spur on his horse and follow if he catches sight of the *mirza's* feather safely waving across the way.*** What is more, if the European narrator is moved to "plumb the depths of existence" by virtue of his experiences in the Crimea, what is to say that the

---

* Alina Witkowska, *Literatura romantzymu* (Warszawa: Państwowy Instytut Wydawniczy, 1987), p. 111.

** Walc, p. 81.

*** See the next sonnet, XVI, "The Mountain Kikineis."

inhabitant of the Crimea, who *lives* at the foot of that "interpreter of God," Chatyrdah, has not already come to an understanding of the frailty of human life vis-à-vis the stability of Nature? After all, it is *he* who, as guide, leads the Pole to the places that inspire him, not vice versa. However Walc may have been inspired to present the Polish narrator as an experienced opponent to Tsarism, in contrast to the naive Tatar: "to him [the Pole] the perspective of history is accessible, which perspective requires the passage of time — after all, Wallenrod doesn't come about with the snap of one's fingers; on the contrary: *One hundred years have passed, since the Knights of the Cross...* And Crimea had been subjugated just yesterday,"* the fact remains that both Tatar *and Pole* are in the same, subject relation to the conquering Russian.

Well, for those of us who have little or nothing invested in the grand questions of Polish heroism and sanctity and independence, in this twenty-first century when (at last) Poland is free, and happy, and the normal European nation it has always longed to be, it is the *Erotic* and *Crimean Sonnets* which may well be the crowning achievement of Adam Mickiewicz, the poet who belongs not only to Poland, but to the world. For in them, he *is* one of us, and not all of us are Poles; he is a man like us, not just an insurrectionist hero or mouthpiece of liberty. Whereas with works like *Forefathers' Eve* or *Konrad Wallenrod* or even *Pan Tadeusz* the person not raised on Polish history and literature needs notes to keep her informed on just what is going on, with the *Sonnets* no such exegesis is necessary. In the *Erotic Sonnets*, Adam Mickiewicz describes the ups and downs of a love affair, from its first timid inception through the bitterness and disillusionment of the final breakup, which is something most of us can relate to; in the *Crimean Sonnets*, Mickiewicz presents us with stunning poetic snapshots of the Crimean Peninsula, speaking to us like a friend returned from abroad, who kindles in us a desire to see with our own eyes the gorgeous surroundings expressed in his art. In short, in approaching the *Sonnets* of Adam Mickiewicz, the Anglophone reader may need the translator as a person to enable him or her to get past the foreign language and into the living, human pith of the "content," traditionally understood, of the poems. But he or she needs little or no scholarly apparatus. The

---

*   Walc, p. 81.

Sonnets of Adam Mickiewicz are one of those great works of literature that strike us as familiar upon the very first reading — it's almost as if we'd read them before. We haven't, but, more importantly, we've *lived* them before; in them, Adam Mickiewicz is executing the primary job of the true poet: putting the reader's own emotions in words, giving voice to things he or she has felt, and would describe to others, if only they could.

ODESSA

And so, one of the greatest works of the greatest poet of Poland was written on Russian soil. The question of how he came to spend an extended period of his life in Crimea, and publish the fruits of his Odessan period in Moscow, has to do with the politics of the times in which he lived. After finishing his studies at the University of Vilnius in 1819, Mickiewicz was certified as a teacher, and sent (in his words) to deal with the "dull heads of Żmudź" in Kowno. While he was at university, Mickiewicz participated in an idealistic fraternity called the Philomatic Brotherhood (*Filomaci*). This group professed general academic aims. However, according to some authors, the fraternity (as well as other student organisations such as the Radiant Society (*Promieniści*) added nationalism and secret revolutionary politics to their programmes. (Historians of the Communist period liked to underscore this fact, emphasising the progressive and anti-establishment nature of the groups whom they saw as fellow travellers *avant la lettre*. Whether or not this was to some extent true, the repressive Tsarist police state was eager to believe it). Mieczysław Jastrun notes:

> After a short period of time they underwent a noticeable evolution: from general goals centring on ethics and self-education to politics and patriotism. Mickiewicz was among the most active of the brotherhood's founders. He laid out the expectations which the Philomats set for themselves in the following words: "The goal of the Fraternity is the good of all, especially as regards the growth of enlightenment as well as the exemplification of the road of enlightenment towards the inculcation of moral values and nationalism." Thus, the goal of

the fraternity was quite broad and capable of including political and revolutionary aims.*

Other authors see the matter differently, understanding the secret nature of some of the club's activities as more indicative of the "simple urge to secrecy proper to youngsters" and the attractive aura of freemason-like societies, rather than serious political intrigue. Thus, early in the twentieth century, Stanisław Tarnowski accepted the presence of a nationalistic strain in the thinking of the Philomats, but differed on their aims and intensity:

> Love of the fatherland, ideal and elevated like all of their sentiments, was their whole spiritual life and the strongest bond between them; yet never was it transformed into activism. It is common knowledge that in none of their societies was there anything really political. Not long ago [*Tarnowski was writing circa 1904*] the last members of the fraternity died, and the best witnesses — Domeyko, Odyniec, and Suzin, all state that even in their most secret thoughts, their most confidential conversations, leanings toward immediate political action never surfaced. An independent, resurrected Poland was of course the goal of all, but any thought of scheduling or organising the means of this resurrection was far from their minds.**

At the time when Tarnowski, to say nothing of Mickiewicz, was writing, Poland did not exist on the map of Europe. Writing his *History of Polish Literature* in the former capital of the Polish kingdom, he was actually living and working in Austrian Krakau. It might be this fact that caused him to paint a more congenial picture of the national bard, with the Imperial censor (though benign, still Austrian, and still wary of revolutionary topics) peering over his shoulder. Jastrun, on the other hand, wrote his short *Life Sketch of Adam Mickiewicz* in the People's Republic of Poland, a satellite of the Soviet Union, and his biography

---

*   Mieczysław Jastrun, *Szkic o Adamie Mickiewiczu* (Warszawa: Wydawnictwo "Polonia", 1956), p. 9.
**   Stanisław Count Tarnowski, *Historya literatury polskiej*, Vol. IV: 'Wiek XIX: 1800-1830' (Kraków: Spółka wydawnicza polska w Krakowie, 1904), p. 263.

at times seems to stress Mickiewicz-Patriot of the People more than Mickiewicz-Poet. Whatever the case may be, as we previously noted, the Tsarist government did suspect something revolutionary in the Philomats' activities, and took action against them.

In 1823, the Tsarist government cracked down on the student organisations at the University of Wilno. Mickiewicz was arrested and imprisoned for nearly six months before being bailed out in April 1824 by the historian and political scientist Joachim Lelewel, his professor and friend. The sentence handed down to him was banishment from the Polish and Lithuanian provinces, a sentence he shared with twenty other Philomats who were exiled into the heart of Russia. For Mickiewicz, it was to be, in the words of fellow Lithuanian poet Czesław Miłosz, "a triumphant exile."*

This can be understood in a wider sense than the mere personal. Walc makes a good case for Mickiewicz's Russian exile being a matter of epochal significance for the development of Polish literature, the Romantic cause in particular:

> Firstly, from the wide horizons of the two Russian capitals, Mickiewicz, who (thanks to Novosiltsov) was sticking his nose beyond the borders of his native Lithuania for the first time, saw things from a new perspective; he was now able to consider the parochial culture of Poland in all its "beauty." He could now see the dangers that threatened Polish culture because of its being walled around in classical rules — in the worst sense of that term — which were propagated by the aesthetical legislators of Warsaw.**

Indeed, finding himself in St. Petersburg in October 1824, Mickiewicz was befriended by the progressive circle of Russian writers who grouped themselves around the journal *Polar Star*. Among them were men of revolutionary temperaments, such as Konrad Ryleev, poet, translator of Byron, and Decembrist. But Mickiewicz did not remain here long. In the winter of 1824 he was sent to Odessa in the company of

---

* Czesław Miłosz, *The History of Polish Literature* (Berkeley and London: University of California Press, 1983), p. 217.

** Walc, p. 71.

two other Poles, dispatched to the Lyceum Richelieu by the Ministry of Education as a French instructor. He never began his classes, however, as it was deemed that such a notoriously revolutionary character might have an unhealthy influence on his pupils. And so, until March 1826, he spent his time in Odessan salons and touring the Crimean peninsula, and it is to this circumstance that we owe the beautiful descriptive power of the *Crimean Sonnets* and much of the adventurous content of the *Erotic* cycle.

THE EROTIC SONNETS

In February of 1825 then, Mickiewicz travelled to Odessa in the company of two other Polish exiles. They immediately found themselves jobless, yet not without change in their pockets for living expenses. The poet spent most of his time amongst the Polish community in Odessa. He was a frequent guest at the salon of Karolina Sobańska, of whom Miłosz writes:

> Karolina [...] was also the mistress of General Witt, chief military commander in southern Russia. [...] She was involved with the Russian secret service, and it seems that her report on the good behaviour of her lover, Mickiewicz, was not without a positive effect on his being granted a passport for travel abroad a few years later. An excursion to the Crimea in the company of General Witt and Mrs Sobańska led Mickiewicz to write his famous *Crimean Sonnets*.*

Miłosz also posits the seemingly alluring Karolina Sobańska as at least one of the heroines of the erotic cycle. Whatever the truth may be in that regard, it is certain that the poet was enjoying himself in the Crimea. In one of his letters to his university chum Tomasz Zan, Mickiewicz remarked that he "was living in Odessa like a pasha."** Franciszek Malewski, one of the other two exiles mentioned above,

---

*   Miłosz, p. 218.
**   Quoted by Adam Rżążewski (Aër), *Mickiewicz w Odessie i twórczość jego z tego czasu* (Warszawa: J. Sikorski, 1898), p. 17.

makes a corroborating statement in a letter to his family: "Mickiewicz says that they pay one here to eat oranges."*

On a more scholarly note, it was in Odessa that Mickiewicz began an earnest study of Italian. In a short time, he was reading the works of Dante and Petrarch in the original, and the spirit of the latter poet is suffused throughout the *Erotic Sonnets*, although he had been familiar with Petrarch since at least 1818.

For, as early as then, he was using the Petrarchan sonnet and the persona of Laura as poetic conceits to express, it is assumed, his grief at his lost love Maryla, back in Lithuania. In "Przypomnienie" ["A Reminder"], the theme of enforced exile and separation of naturally-inclined hearts is already struck, which was to come to powerful fruition in Crimean Sonnet XIV, "Pielgrzym" ["The Pilgrim"]:

> Ona w lubej dziedzinie, która mi odjęta,
> Gdzie jej wszystko o wiernym powiada kochanku —
> Depcąc świeże me ślady czyż o mnie pamięta?

> [She, in that beloved region, of which I was deprived, / where everything speaks to her of a faithful lover — treading in my fresh traces, does she remember me?]

But there are two heroines to be found in the erotic cycle. The first, as mentioned above, is traditionally supposed to be Maryla Wereszczakówna, the poet's first flame from his student days in Polish Lithuania. The second we know only as "D.D." As that first love was thwarted by an arranged marriage, the second — although there are hints that it was consummated — was thwarted too, by the woman's marital status.

Nine of the twenty two *Erotic Sonnets* are dedicated to the Maryla/Laura-figure, eleven to "D.D.," one to women in general, and one to the poet's critics.

In the style of the period, the sonnets dedicated to Maryla/Laura are for the most part sweetly melancholic sighs, fourteen lines long, in the classical thirteen-syllable Polish verse line. In the first sonnet, the seemingly nostalgic poet reminisces about his first meeting with his love:

---

*   Quoted by Rżążewski, p. 7.

> Ledwieś piosnkę zaczęła, jużem łzy uronił:
> Twój głos wnikał do serca i za duszę chwytał;
> Zdało się, że ją anioł po imieniu witał,
> I w zegar niebios chwilę zbawienia zadzwonił.
>
> [You'd barely begun your song, and already I was weeping; / your voice penetrated my heart and grasped hold of my soul; / It seemed that an angel was greeting her by name, / and the clocktower of the heavens sounded the moment of salvation.]

This same strain of longing may be further exemplified by the final lines of number VIII, in which the poet thus addresses the river Niemen:

> Kędy jest miłe latek dziecinnych wesele?
>
> Gdzie milsze burzliwego wieku niepokoje?
> Kędy jest Laura moja, gdzie są przyjaciele?
> Wszystko przeszło, a czemuż nie przejdą łzy moje!
>
> [Where are the pleasant joys of my childhood years? // Where are the even more pleasant anxieties of my stormy age? // Where is my Laura, where are my friends? / Everything's passed away, but why will my tears not pass away?]

The fact of the poet's exile had a pronounced effect on the composition of the erotic sonnets, as well as those of the Crimean cycle. Stanisław Tarnowski, among others, has made note of the theme of yearning found in them:

> In nearly all of them, even in such as express moments of happiness, a deep longing is to be found, which sometimes lightens, but always remains the spiritual background. It has two objects […] one of which is his old love, for his past lover, […] as painful as a wound that has barely scarred over, […] while the second is Lithuania, his dear homeland.*

---

*   Tarnowski, p. 330.

Kuziak notes this same characteristic, and takes it a step further in his chapter devoted to "Longing and Trauma:"

> It is proper to note here the significance of memory in Mickiewicz's ontology. On the one hand, it constitutes the identity of the subject, formed with the passage of time. On the other, it appears marked with traumatic experiences, destructive of the ego.*

While it is true that the figure of the narrator becomes extremely submerged in the atmosphere that surrounds him — whether that be the narrator of the erotic cycle, completely lost in the will and charm of the beloved, or the intrepid traveller of the Crimean cycle, transformed by the beauty of his surroundings into a voracious eye — his "ego" is only suspended, not destroyed. It emerges at the end of the erotic cycle with his bitter denunciation of womankind (who knocked him down, but could not bury him), as it does at the end of the Crimean cycle, with his triumphant self-paean of victory over his critics, in the confident style of Horace's *Exegi monumentum aere perennius*.

Kuziak — perhaps this is because the critic himself is the product of the twentieth / twenty-first centuries, the philosophy of which is characterised by a subjectivity and a relativism unchained from its moorings — muses often, not on the poet's interaction with his surroundings, but on his creation of the same in the world of his writing:

> In consequence, the subjectivity of the sonnets is not a phenomenon preceding the language and expressing itself in language [...] as biographical allusion would suggest, but rather comes to be in the world of the text itself, presenting the trace, not of a real person, but of itself.**

In contradistinction to this poetic self-creation through writing, Alina Witkowska concentrates on Mickiewicz's fascination with the

---

*   Kuziak, p. 41.
** Kuziak, p. 87.

concrete (and thus, with a reality that exists outside of the author and his compositions, informing — and shaping — both):

> In the *Crimean Sonnets* one finds a confirmation of the general thesis touching upon the aesthetics of the romantic landscape, which — in contrast to that of the classicists — is based upon the concrete: on the characteristic, on the respect for the difference fixed in nature and perceived by the vigilant eye of the perceiver.*

As far as the dispersion of the individual, so to speak, is concerned, it might be said that the poet submerges himself stylistically, in homage to Petrarch, and this, at times, takes the form of outright translation. Indeed, five of the Polish sonnets are based more or less on those of the Italian master: I ("Erano i capei d'oro a l'aura sparsi"); IV ("Per mezz' i boschi inospiti e selvaggi"); V ("S'amor non è, chè dunque è quel ch'io sento?"); VII "Senuccio, i' vo' che sappi, in qual maniera); X ("Quando fra l'altre donne ad ora ad ora"). Similarly, sonnets XV—XVII from the erotic cycle may well be built around Petrarch's "La sera desiar, odiar l'aurora."

Books are made of other books, as Eliot was wont to say. Whether translations, adaptations, or inspired offspring of Petrarch's work, the love sonnets of Adam Mickiewicz are anything but slavish imitations of source-texts. One of the important ways in which Mickiewicz differs from his Italian master is in his sense of humour. Even number II, in which the poet feelingly expresses the contrary impulses of righteous wrath and boundless forgiveness, which wrestle for control in the wronged lover's breast, is not devoid of a humorous, mocking self-irony:

> Mówię z sobą, z drugimi plączę się w rozmowie;
> Serce bije gwałtownie, oddechem nie władnę;
> Iskry czuję w źrenicach, a na twarzy bladnę;
> Niejeden z obcych głośno pyta o me zdrowie,
>
> Albo o mym rozumie coś na ucho powie.

---

*   Witkowska, p. 110.

[I talk to myself, and speak confusedly in conversations with others; / my heart beats violently, I cannot control my breathing; / I feel sparks in my eyes, while my face grows pale; / More than one of the strangers [around me] inquires loudly about my health, // or whispers something about my mental state into someone's ear.]

The lightheartedness becomes bitter wit in "Widzenie się w gaju" ["Meeting in the Grove"]. That sonnet describes the nighttime tryst of two lovers, of whom the woman is troubled by scruples. The male narrator reacts to his love's *mea culpa* with searing sarcasm:

Przebóg! jesteśmyż winni, że siedzimy społem!

Wszak siedzę tak daleko, mówię tak niewiele,
I zabawiam się z tobą, mój ziemski aniele!
Jak gdybyś już niebieskim stała się aniołem.

[For God's sake! Are we guilty of sitting together! // After all, I sit so far away, and I say so little / and I deal with you, my earthly angel! / As if you'd already become an angel in heaven."]

Thus, the reader expecting the usual hearts-and-flowers love poetry may just be disappointed in the *Erotic Sonnets* of Adam Mickiewicz. But this is, ironically, their strongest point, artistically speaking. Although Tarnowski is correct in his assessment that, similar to Jan Kochanowski's *Laments* on the death of his daughter, the *Erotic Sonnets* present a whole sequence of emotional experiences, in which "an entire, common story of erotic intrigue is contained, from the first beat of the heart and the first sweet anxiety to the final bitterness and distaste,"* it can also be said that they are love sonnets in which love plays a relatively minor role — the sardonic focus is almost entirely on the psychological state of the lover himself. The hackneyed theme of unrequited love does not give way to a morbid, purple brooding, but is rather the vehicle for some of the most delightful, ironic humour east of Byron. For example, number XV:

---

*   Tarnowski, p. 332.

> Dzieńdobry! już westchnęła, błysnął promyk w oku,
> Dzieńdobry! już obraża światłość twe źrenice,
> Naprzykrzają się ustom muchy swawolnice,
> Dzieńdobry! słońce w oknach, ja przy twoim boku.
>
> [Good morning! Now she's sighed, a ray of sunlight has flashed in her eye, / Good morning! Now the light irritates her eyes, / and wanton flies buzzing round her lips annoy her, / Good morning! The sun is at the window, and I am by your side.]

But if he might playfully consider himself a pest to his beloved on the order of pesky flies awakened by the dawning Southern sun, the torment he himself has to undergo from her frivolous, polite reception of the dull trains of daily visitors is described as something out of his other Crimean lecture, the *Inferno*:

> Gdybym mógł, progi wilczą otoczyłbym jamą,
> Stawiłbym lisie pastki, kolczate okowy,
> A jeśli nie dość bronią, uciec bym gotowy
> Na tamten świat, stygową zasłonić się tamą.
>
> O przeklęty nudziarzu! ja liczę minuty,
> Jak zbrodniarz, co go czeka ostatnia katusza:
> Ty pleciesz błahe dzieje wczorajszej reduty.
>
> [If I could, I'd surround [your] threshold with a wolves' den, / fox traps, sharp bear traps, / and if weapons were not enough, I'd be ready to escape / into the next world, to protect [us] with a Stygian barrier. // O you damned bore! I count the minutes, / like a criminal awaiting his execution: / while you mumble through a report of the meaningless events of yesterday's ball.]

The poet casts love aside at the end of this cycle of love sonnets, which comes as the culmination of a progressive refusal to allow centre stage to any other person save himself. It is a brilliant formal preparation for that truly splendid portion of his sonneteering, the *Crimean Sonnets*. For the cycle finishes with two liberating rejections. In number XXI, Mickiewicz's narrator frees himself convincingly from the tyranny of wasting immortal verse on (and to) the empty, frivolous women to whom he has hitherto made his muse subservient* — in one of the most angry verses in Polish literature, women have become nothing more than "Danaïds" in the eyes of their one-time votary. Then, in the very next sonnet, "Ekskuza" ["Apologia"], which brings the erotic cycle to a close, the poet aims his darts at his contemporary critics, who, in turn, castigated him for abandoning elevated themes worthy of a national bard to piddle about with silly love intrigues. In a strong, evocative symbolic image, the bard snaps the strings of his lyre and flings it into the river Lethe. From now on, in the best Romantic fashion, he will write for no one save himself — he will neither try to please women with expertise in love, or classicists with his mastery of form. Like Aeneas on the night he left Carthage, Mickiewicz slices the mooring cables of his ship and sets out without looking back. His decision was to result in one of the most unique poetic creations of the romantic period.

THE CRIMEAN SONNETS

Mickiewicz set out from Odessa on 29 August 1825 (17 August, Old Style) for a three-month-long tour of the Crimean Peninsula in the company of the Sobański family and other members of the Odessan Polish community. Adam Rżążewski, true to the period in which he was writing, perhaps, ascribes such noble motives to the journey:

> In order to pull the poet out of his moral depression [*i.e. the lows following the affair with D.D.*]; in order to ease the bitterness at heart caused by this blow to his sensitive nature, as well as to stanch the spiteful gossip which was already beginning to circulate, the Sobańskis, along with Henryk Rzewuski, proposed a caravan tour through Crimea.**

Among other tourists accompanying the poet on this voyage were General Witt and a shady fellow named Aleksander Boszniak. Stanisław Makowski suggests that these latter-named gentlemen had

---

*   As Walc reminds us, the *Sonnets* are the last love poems that he was ever to write. pp. 82-83.

**   Rżążewski, p. 34.

other matters beside the poet's emotional health in mind. Witt, he informs us, was most likely using the journey as a pretext to survey the lay of the land in preparation for the announced visit of Tsar Aleksander I to the southern provinces of his empire. Boszniak, who was to play a rather shameful role in the rounding up of the Southern Union conspiracy, was also to keep his eyes and ears open. And, as Miłosz has already reminded us, "Madame Sobańska busied herself with denunciation for Witt as well, and more than once supplied him with important 'observations and news.'"*

Heartbreak, spies, a poet, the exotic South… all we need is a murder and a few spectres to complete a plot worthy of the worst Gothic penny dreadful. It gets even better when one considers the suppositions made by some concerning Mickiewicz's own "real motives" for the journey. Was the handsome, heart-wounded young Romantic a secret agent of the Decembrists, conspiring the overthrow of a tyrannic Tsar? Unfortunately (or perhaps fortunately), there are no documents to support this claim apart from a few obscure letters written by known Russian conspirators. What is important is this: whether the poet had a political agenda or not, the cycle of eighteen descriptive sonnets which he was to compose during the course of the trip were to outlive any sort of politics.

Having freed himself of emotional baggage, Mickiewicz set about transforming the sonnet into a powerful descriptive tool of photographic brilliance. The visual nature of the sonnets is underlined in a curious reminiscence of one of the poet's fellow travellers, who spoke thus of the cycle's genesis:

> [Mickiewicz] couldn't draw to save his life. He took up the pencil, however, and attempted to put down on paper what he saw before him. It seemed to him that since he so perfectly felt the beauties he looked upon, technical difficulties shouldn't stand in his way. […] We had the opportunity to examine a few of these drawings of his, and, looking at them, one might well burst out in gay laughter. There is something of the fantastic in these figures — they have the appearance of drawings traced on sand by small children. […] There was great joy among

---

*   Makowski, pp. 12-13.

his fellow voyagers when Mr Kałusowski, who accompanied the poet on horseback one day, related to Madame Sobańska in confidence that "Adam entrusted him with his horse, lay down on his belly on the soft moss just like a shepherd, and surrounded by the thick bent grass, began writing something non-stop, in a tiny hand, on small slips of paper."*

A failed attempt at drawing, then, was the beginning of one of the most striking literary creations of the nineteenth century, a cycle of sonnets that one modern critic was to call an "explosion of vision" of a poet, whose "voracious eye reflected natural phenomena and landscapes"** in a completely new and brilliant fashion. For even in those sonnets which speak of the last tatters of love, even in those in which the observed phenomena awaken bitter reflections of his exile status, it is the phenomena themselves, the natural wonders and ruins of the Crimean Peninsula, which are ever in the forefront. The dominating emotion of this cycle is the poet's almost childlike joy in perceiving his surroundings. Like the drawings or paintings with which he originally intended to catalogue his journey, the *Crimean Sonnets* are above all visual masterpieces, in which any political or romantic message is of secondary importance to the sensory immediacy, the physical presence in which the poet finds himself, and in which he engulfs the reader.

This subsuming of the poet in the physical surroundings of the awe-inspiring peninsula can be seen even in sonnets that ostensibly deal with the same subject matter as the erotic cycle: separation from a beloved woman, and a beloved homeland:

> Litwo! piały mi wdzięczniej twe szumiące lasy
> Niż słowiki Bajdaru, Salhiry dziewice;
> I weselszy deptałem twoje trzęsawice
> Niż rubinowe morwy, złote ananasy.
>
> [Lithuania! your soughing forests sang more gracefully to me / than the nightingales of Baidar and the maidens of Salhira;

---

*   Rżążewski, pp. 71, 72.
**   Witkowska, p. 110.

/ and more gaily did I tread your bogs / than ruby-coloured mulberries, and golden pineapples.]

There is a significant difference between this verse of love-longing and comparable sonnets found in the erotic cycle. The earlier cycle is no less perceptively concrete in its imagery than the *Crimean Sonnets*. However, there, the concrete phenomena related by the poet are for the most part the stock and stuff of romantic lyrics: balls and soirées, a bedroom door closed before the nose of the pursuing lover, groves, roses, "Laura" … in short, they are of the same order as that found in the cantos of Pushkin's *Evgeny Onegin*. And as in that Russian masterpiece, the realia are subservient to the theme: they provide a satisfying backdrop for the amusing, introspective lover and his gallery of beauties. In the *Crimean Sonnets*, on the other hand, it is the reflective theme and musings that are a background to the striking, fresh material surroundings. As in the fragment from sonnet number XIV quoted above, Mickiewicz is really luxuriating in the voluptuous images and exotic, legendary allure of the Black Sea region, and is using themes such as broken hearts and an exile's loneliness as a structure, a vehicle, an excuse to daub his literary canvases with the passionate, exotic colours of the South.

Nowhere is this hedonistic, aesthetic pleasure more vividly present than in the sextet from number XII:

> Usypiam pod skrzydłami ciszy i ciemnoty;
> Wtem budzą mię rażące meteoru błyski,
> Niebo, ziemię i góry oblał potop złoty!
>
> Nocy wschodnia! ty na kształt wschodniej odaliski
> Pieszczotami usypiasz, a kiedym snu bliski,
> Ty iskrą oka znowu budzisz do pieszczoty.
>
> [I fall asleep beneath the wings of silence and darkness; / then the blazing sparkle of a meteor wakes me, / heaven and earth and mountains are bathed in a golden flood! // O eastern night! Like an oriental odalisque / you soothe to sleep with caresses, and then, when sleep is close / with the spark of your eye you wake one for further caresses.]

This effusiveness is not altogether that of the enraptured tourist. Just as Mickiewicz strove to emulate Petrarch in his collection of hard-luck love sonnets, so in his cycle of Eastern descriptive sonnets he consciously patterned his phrasing after what he took to be Oriental tropes. This is something that, marginally speaking, would not be pleasing to the classicists back at home. In sonnet V, "A View of Mountains from the Kozlov Steppes," the self-styled pilgrim enthuses:

> Tam? czy Allah postawił ścianą morze lodu?
> Czy aniołom tron odlał z zamrożonej chmury?
> Czy Diwy z ćwierci lądu dźwignęli te mury,
> Aby gwiazd karawanę nie puszczać ze wschodu?
>
> [There? Did Allah set up a sea of ice as a wall? / Did He pour a throne for the angels from frozen cloud? / Did Divon raise those walls from a quarter part of the earth / So as to forbid the caravan of the stars ingress from the east?]

In this, the poet is attempting to mimic the metaphorical usage of Eastern speech, as described by Józef Sękowski, the nineteenth-century Polish Orientalist whose book *Collectanea* Mickiewicz had with him on his voyage:

> The European speaking in Persian or Turkish is most often immediately recognised among Orientals from the very manner in which he paints his feelings. Each one of us would say: "That house is large — huge." An Easterner, on the other hand, looking at that same building, would immediately exclaim "That edifice touches heaven — higher it reaches than the firmament!" — although this latter expression carries no more meaning in his mind than the former.*

Yet Mickiewicz is no dilettante. He is aware of the artificiality of his linguistic game, and expresses his awareness of it in a vein of self-irony. This poem is one of the "dialogue-sonnets," in which two distinct voices are heard: that of the "pilgrim," Mickiewicz's narrator, and that

---

*   Quoted by Makowski, p. 103.

of his *mirza*, or Persian guide. Just after this bit of manneristic (though nonetheless real) enthusiasm, the *mirza* responds in authentic Eastern hyperbole, after which the pilgrim can reply with nothing more than an astounded "Aah!!," expressing his awe at the *mirza's* beautiful turn of phrase no less than the grandeur of the scenery.

Now, it would be unjust to suggest that Mickiewicz was merely striking a pose when extrapolating moral lessons from the scenery in which he was surrounded, as in the case of the supposed tomb of Maria Potocka (a young Polish heiress sold into slavery among the Crimean Tatars). Whether or not he knew that the legend was doubtful at best,* we have no right to assume that his reflections on the exile's grave awaiting him were but empty, pedantic phrases. Similarly, the quasi-biblical assurance of the temporality of earthly kingdoms expressed in "Bakchysarai," is not just a pleasant vacation snapshot, it can be, as Walc suggests, the poet's comment on contemporary empires — the Russian, in particular.

The *Crimean Sonnets* are brought to a conclusion by the confident verse "Ajudah." This sonnet, like "Apologia," concerns itself with the poet and his work. Unlike the latter verse, however, with its biting tone, "Ajudah" is quietly triumphant. Speaking of the pearl-strewing waves he gazes upon, the narrator muses:

> Podobnie na twe serce, O poeto młody!
> Namiętność często groźne wzburza niepogody,
> Lecz gdy podniesziesz bardon, ona bez twej szkody
>
> Ucieka w zapomnienia pogrążyć sie toni
> I nieśmiertelne pieśni za sobą uroni,
> Z których wieki uplotą ozdobę twych skroni.
>
> [This is like your heart, O young poet! / Passion often brews up dangerous bad weather, / but when you take up your lute, [that passion] without having harmed you / retreats to sink into oblivion / leaving behind it immortal songs, / from which the ages shall weave an adornment for your brow.]

---

*   As he admits in his "Clarifications," however half-heartedly.

While we are here, it is worth taking note of Jan Walc's interesting theory — which he bases on the frequent allusions made to flight in the *Sonnets* — that the Crimean voyage was a process of growth, both poetical and political, for the poet. Speaking of the sonnet before us now, he notes:

> And that's why the dramatic, spiritually speaking, journey to Crimea finds its culmination in the hieratic image of the poet leaning against the Judah cliff; this is now a completely different person from him, who journeyed to Crimea through the Akerman steppes — from the Crimea, it is not a youth, but a mature man, who is returning.

Similarly, on the same page Walc considers the stoic loneliness of the narrator of sonnet nr. IV, "Storm," to be an expression, not of Byronic heroism, but political independence: "[Here] Mickiewicz attains independence, a liberation from paralysing fear."* Alina Witkowska, on the other hand, perhaps more convincingly, emphasises the poetical development that took place in the young poet's life thanks to the Crimean voyage. As she sees it,

> The *Crimean Sonnets* are permeated with a victorious, one might even say provocative, tendency to the breaking of linguistic barriers. He harnesses his tongue to descriptive functions, urges it to operations to which, up until then, it was unaccustomed.**

With this poem, leaning upon Judah cliff, the poet's journey, the literal trip over the peninsula and the no less important maturing of his verse over the space of these forty-odd sonnets, is complete. The self-assuredness won by the poet is evident in a letter written by Mickiewicz to his mentor Joachim Lelewel:

> Did I ever experience the Crimea! I held out through a rough sea-gale and was one of a handful of healthy folk who retained

---

*   Walc, p. 81.
**   Witkowska, p. 111.

enough strength and consciousness to glut their eyes with the interesting sights. I trod the clouds on Chatyrdah (most likely the Trapeza of the ancients); slept on the Girei's sofas and played chess with the porter of the late Khan in a laurel-hung verandah. I saw the East in miniature. What remains of my memories will be found in the *Sonnets*.*

THIS TRANSLATION

Just as most bass players first learn the guitar, most translators of verse have written their own poetry before turning their hand to translation. There may be those who have translated poems in prose, or line-by-line, for use in a scholarly paper they were writing, but true verse translation, when the translator is striving to recreate the form and content, the "gists and piths" in the words of Ezra Pound, of the original poem in a new language, is always the product of a person who had been a poet first, and then turned his hand to translation.

So, certainly, it is with me. Whether or not I deserve to be called a poet, or the products of my pen poetry, is not for me to say. However, in my case, the chicken certainly came before the egg: I first delighted in stringing words together in original compositions, and only later, when I had begun to learn other languages, and to find great pleasure reading them, would I come across something that so delighted me, that I was moved to attempt its recreation in my own idiom.

I say this, because these *Sonnets of Adam Mickiewicz* are the closest things to original compositions among all of the translations I have ever done. I do not know whether those who are interested in translation as a craft, or those who enjoy comparing translations to the originals, will consider them adaptations rather than translations; that, I believe, is a matter of semantics. My *Sonnets* present the reader with the "information" provided by Mickiewicz himself, and I do not perform any wild formal acrobatics — the very form of the sonnet is rather prohibitive in this regard. (Still, there are one or two places where, for effect, I abandon the traditional form; the reader will judge whether or not I was justified in doing so). What I would say is that the idea of poetic inspiration, the feeling that one gets when one is in

---

*   Letter to Lelewel, January, 1827.

the grip of an idea and the poetic formulation that flows therefrom, in an almost uncanny way, is a real thing — and during the translation of these sonnets, I had just such an experience that is usually reserved for original compositions.

The careful reader will question my assertion above concerning the slightness of my departure from the "rather prohibitive" sonnet form. Throughout the sonnets, Mickiewicz was true to Petrarchan form (ABBA, ABBA, and some form of CDC DCD for the sextets), while I have not been so faithful. Most often, the quatrains of these translations run ABBA CDDC, or some variation thereof; I hope that this departure will not be so irksome to the reader as to impair his enjoyment of the book.

Purists will bitch and moan, as purists do, and give this little book a scornful shove. But when we're talking fresh rhyme-words for "love," I haven't got that many. How about you? Donne has been gone since 1632, or he might be appealed to — hand in glove, he, and Petrarchan form! Each quatrain grew out of the former, flawless. He marched in where Shakespeare feared to tread, and won the day. The neither fish-nor-fowl scheme of my verse — will it be mimicked in some latter day? And called (perhaps) the "Sonnet Crascevschian?" (Unless they choose to call it something worse…)

All joking aside, are these English poems, then, more Kraszewski than Mickiewicz? Again, that is not for me to say. However, because of the very idiosyncratic nature of many, if not all, of these translations, I have added "literal" prose translations of each of the sonnets to the Notes section of the book. In this, I am following the advice of that greatest of all modern theoreticians of translation, George Steiner, who posits that the verse translation: a) ought to be an attempt at recreating the original in the target language, in such a way that it appears to be a native growth; b) should have the original facing it, for reasons of comparison; and c) ought to be outfitted in explanatory notes describing the translator's difficulties and choices. My prose addenda and notes ought to serve the same purpose as a prose paraphrase, which, in Steiner's words, "perhaps bracketing the principal difficulties, should fill the margin as in a polyglot Bible."* The prototype of this

---

*   George Steiner, *The Penguin Book of Modern Verse Translation* (Middlesex: Penguin, 1966), p. 35.

sort of translation, in his view, is Vladimir Nabokov's four-volume presentation of Pushkin's *Evgeny Onegin*. While I do not go as far as Nabokov in trying to lay bare the essence of my work, it is my hope that these prose trots in the notes will be of some aid to those readers who would like to separate the Kraszewski chaff from the Mickiewicz grain, or for those who may be more interested in the Polish originals, but need a crutch to deal with them. In any case, I hope the reader finds this translation worth her while.

As always, "the disciple is never above his master." Thus, whatever beauties the English reader finds in my translations of Mickiewicz's *Sonnets*, I unabashedly and with no false modesty attribute to the genius of the Polish bard, apologising at the same time both to You, gentle reader, and You, Adam, for the many rough-spots and bumbles they necessarily contain — faults of my clumsy pen alone.

ACKNOWLEDGEMENTS

I would like to thank everyone at Glagoslav for their continuing faith in my work; in particular, my editor Ksenia Papazova, and all the copy-editors and typesetters for their keen eyes and suggestions. As always, I am most grateful to my wife Ola for many years of love and support unclouded by the least sort of discord or heartache described in some of these poems.

Miami Beach
11 May 2018

Adam Mickiewicz

Sonety miłosne / The Erotic Sonnets

Quand'era in parte altr'uom da quel, ch'io sono.

Today I am not what I used to be.
—Petrarch

I
DO LAURY

Ledwiem ciebie zobaczył, jużem się zapłonił,
W nieznanem oku dawnej znajomości pytał;
I z twych jagód wzajemny rumieniec wykwitał,
Jak z róży, której piersi zaranek odsłonił.

Ledwieś piosnkę zaczęła, jużem łzy uronił:
Twój głos wnikał do serca i za duszę chwytał;
Zdało się, że ją anioł po imieniu witał,
I w zegar niebios chwilę zbawienia zadzwonił.

O luba! niech twe oczy przyznać się nie boją!
Jeśli cię mem spójrzeniem, jeśli głosem wzruszę:
Nie dbam, że los i ludzie przeciwko nam stoją,

Że uciekać i kochać bez nadziei muszę!
Niech ślub ziemski innego darzy ręką twoją,
Tylko wyznaj, że Bóg mi poślubił twą duszę!

I
TO LAURA

At your first glance I felt love's crimson glow,
In first-met eyes I sought some time-worn bond;
On your cheeks too, a blush — as when the dawn
Lays bare the soft breasts of a youthful rose.

Unused to weep, still tears welled in my eyes,
Your words so flushed the heart and soul enflamed;
It seemed some angel greeted her by name
And Time's Great Hour tolled in the breaking skies.

O Love! Shame not your telling eyes with "Crime!"
Should I with glance or song approach your heart;
So men and destiny against us stand,

And I, hopeless for now, must stand apart …

O, earthly vows grant someone else your hand —
Yet grant me this: God spoused your soul with mine!

II

Mówię z sobą, z drugimi plączę się w rozmowie;
Serce bije gwałtownie, oddechem nie władnę;
Iskry czuję w źrenicach, a na twarzy bladnę;
Niejeden z obcych głośno pyta o me zdrowie,

Albo o mym rozumie cóś na ucho powie.
Tak cały dzień przemęczę. Gdy na łoże padnę,
W nadziei że snem chwilę cierpieniom ukradnę,
Serce ogniste mary zapala w mej głowie.

Zrywam się, biegę, składam na pamięć wyrazy,
Któremi mam złorzeczyć okrucieństwu twemu,
Składane, zapomniane, po milijon razy.

Ale gdy ciebie ujrzę, nie pojmuję czemu
Znowu jestem spokojny, zimniejszy nad głazy,
Aby goreć na nowo — milczeć po dawnemu...

II

I talk to myself.
                            And stutter as well.
My heart beats like bullies, I wheeze like a horse,
I've sparks in my pupils, a face like a corpse;
(Some old prune, loudly: "That young man — is he *well?*")

Someone whispers "cuckoo" while winking at me…
And thus my waking life. Still worse in bed,
Where burning visions sear my thrashing head,
In vain I seek to steal some peace from sleep.

Up again, pacing. I rote-learn odium
With which to call to heel your brutishness,
Words dripping venom!…
                            soon of venom dry
With just the sight of you. For God knows why
I'm peaceful again — as cold as stone — and just
To flame up fresh — like always — and hold my tongue.

III

Nieuczona twa postać, niewymyślne słowa,
Ani lice, ni oko nad inne nie błyska:
A każdy rad cię ujrzeć, rad posłyszeć z bliska.
Choć w ubraniu pasterki, widno żeś królowa.

Wczora brzmiały i pieśni i głośna rozmowa,
Pytano się o twoich rówiennic nazwiska;
Ten im pochwały sypie, inny żarty ciska;
Ty weszłaś, — każdy święte milczenie zachowa.

Tak śród uczty, gdy śpiewak do choru wyzywał,
Gdy koła tańcujących wiły się po sali:
Nagle staną i zmilkną; każdy zapytywał,

Nikt nie wiedział dlaczego w zadumieniu stali.
„Ja wiem, rzecze poeta, anioł przelatywał."
Uczcili wszyscy gościa, — nie wszyscy poznali.

III

Unpolished your bearing, your speech unveneered,
What is there in you to explain your sway?
You show — departing guests decide to stay,
Retire — at once the buzzing floor is cleared.

Last night, amidst laughter, song, and champagne spilled,
Dull dinnerjackets "Charmed, I'm sure"d plain girls,
Reeked gentility, sneered at fellow-churls…
You entered, and this hive of trifles stilled.

Thus at a feast, where song laughs through the air
And blushing dancers wheel about the hall,
The riot stops
              as if on cue, but why?…
All ask, with shoulders shrugged, blank stares…
Until the bard: "A god just now passed by."
Sensed, spilt to, yet unrecognised by all.

IV
WIDZENIE SIĘ W GAJU

*„Tyżeś to? i tak późno?..." „Błędną miałem drogę
Śród lasów, przy niepewnym księżyca promyku.
Tęskniłaś? myślisz o mnie?..." „Luby niewdzięczniku!
Pytaj się czy ja myśleć o czem innem mogę!"*

*„Pozwól uścisnąć dłonie, ucałować nogę.
Ty drżysz! czego?..." „Ja nie wiem. Błądząc po gaiku,
Lękam się szmeru liścia, nocnych ptaków krzyku:
Ach! musimy być winni, kiedy czujem trwogę!"*

*„Spójrzyj mi w oczy, w czoło: nigdy z takiem czołem
Nie idzie zbrodnia, trwoga nie patrzy tak śmiele.
Przebóg! jesteśmyż winni, że siedzimy społem!*

*„Wszak siedzę tak daleko, mówię tak niewiele,
I zabawiam się z tobą, mój ziemski aniele!
Jak gdybyś już niebieskim stała się aniołem."*

IV
MEETING IN THE GROVE

"Is it you? So late!" "Sorry…I got lost,
With the moon so dim, and trees all around;
Did you miss … think of me?" "Ungrateful clown!
As if my head held any other thoughts!"

"Here, give me your hand — or your foot to kiss…
You're shaking! Why?" — "I don't know — waiting here
Bird-cries and leaves rustling fill me with fear —
This must be a sin if we're trembling like this!"

"Stop it! Look in these eyes — crime never pairs
With such calm! And since when is fright so bold?
God! We're guilty of sitting together?

At each end of the bench — alone, rather!
O my earthly angel! My suit so fares
As if you really were so blest and cold!"

V

Potępi nas świętoszek, rozpustnik wyśmieje,
Że chociaż samotnemi otoczeni ściany,
Chociaż ona tak młoda, ja tak zakochany,
Przecież ja oczy spuszczam, a ona łzy leje.

Ja bronię się ponętom; ona i nadzieje
Chce odstraszyć, co chwila brząkając kajdany,
Któremi ręce związał nam los opłakany.
Nie wiemy sami, co się w sercach naszych dzieje.

Jestże to ból lub rozkosz? Gdy czuję ściśnienia
Twych dłoni, kiedy z ustek zachwycę płomienia:
Luba! czyż mogę temu dać imię cierpienia?

Ale kiedy się łzami nasze lica zroszą,
Gdy się ostatki życia w westchnieniach unoszą:
Luba: czyliż to mogę nazywać rozkoszą?

V

The sneering prude damns us, the smirking rake jeers,
That though but four walls and ceiling above
Surround her so young and me so beloved,
I stare at the floor — she's always in tears.

I beat back allurement — as she does all hope,
At each of our meetings — in public, at trysts —
By rattling the chains that bind fast our wrists.
What our own hearts intend is beyond our scope…

Is this pain, or delight? Your hands in mine,
Our trembling lips burning with passion bright,
Love! Dare I brand this heaven *suffering*?

But when our eyes are swollen with sobbing,
When we breathe out life's dregs in hopeless sighs,
O Love! Can I then name this hell *delight*?

VI
RANEK I WIECZÓR

Słońce błyszczy na wschodzie w chmur ognistych wianku,
A na zachodzie księżyc blade lice mroczy,
Róża za słońcem pączki rozwinione toczy,
Fijołek klęczy zgięty pod kroplami ranku.

Laura błysnęła w oknie. Ukląkłem na ganku;
Ona, muskając sploty swych złotych warkoczy,
„Czemu," rzekła, „tak rano smutne macie oczy,
I miesiąc i fijołek, i ty, mój kochanku?"

W wieczór przyszedłem nowym bawić się widokiem:
Wraca księżyc, twarz jego pełna i rumiana,
Fijołek podniósł listki orzeźwione mrokiem:

Znowu stanęła w oknie moja ukochana,
W piękniejszym jeszcze stroju i z weselszem okiem;
Znowu u nóg jej klęczę — tak smutny jak z rana.

VI
MORNING AND EVENING

The rising sun is wreathed in flaming clouds,
The westing moon fades with its bloodless cheek;
The blossoming rosebuds wake, and seek
Light; dew-laden, the violet kneels bowed.

Then I glimpsed Laura — on my knees I fell
Before her shining window. "Why" (she frowned,
Braiding her hair) "these sad faces all around —
The moon's, the violet's, and my Love's as well?"

That evening — I'm at her window once more —
The moon returns, face rosy and robust;
The violet stands upright, sobered by the dusk;

Again my Love stands in the window nigh
In gayer garb and with yet gayer eyes;
I'm on my knees again, sad like before.

VII
Z PETRARKI

Senuccio i' vo' che sappi

Chcecie wiedzieć, co cierpię, rówiennicy moi?
Odmaluję najwierniej, ile pióro zdoła.
Mary ja dotąd pośród pamiątek kościoła
Myślą gonię i duch mój o przeszłości roi.

Tu zwykła igrać, ówdzie zamyślona stoi,
Tam z niechęcią twarz kryła, tu mię okiem woła,
Tu gniewna, tam posępna, tu znowu wesoła,
Tu swe lica w łagodność, tu w powagę stroi.

Tam piosenkę nuciła, tu mi dłoń ścisnęła,
Tu usiadła, tam naszej rozmowy początek.
Stąd biegła, tu na piasku imię moje kryśli,

Tam słówko powiedziała, tu z cicha westchnęła,
Tam się zarumieniła—ach! śród tych pamiątek
Wiecznie miota się serce i plączą się myśli.

VII
FROM PETRARCH

What is this pain that grips me so, you ask?
I'll show you, if my pen can paint at all:
Each day, through memory's labyrinthine halls
My soul runs after phantoms from the past.

Here she would play — there she paced thoughtfully,
There scorned me sharply, here called me with her eye,
Here angry — gloomy — laughing with delight;
Cheeks paling proudly — colouring mildly.

There she breathed out a song, here squeezed my hand,
Here she sat down, there our first words were spoke,
She fled this place, traced names here in the sand,

There she said something, and here sighed silently,
There she blushed… Ha! among these memories
And tangled thoughts my heart forever gropes.

VIII
DO NIEMNA

Niemnie, domowa rzeko moja! gdzie są wody,
Które niegdyś czerpałem w niemowlęce dłonie,
Na których potem w dzikie pływałem ustronie,
Sercu niespokojnemu szukając ochłody?

Tu Laura, patrząc z chlubą na cień swej urody,
Lubiła włos zaplatać i zakwiecać skronie,
Tu obraz jej malowny w srebrnej fali łonie
Łzami nieraz mąciłem, zapaleniec młody.

Niemnie, domowa rzeko, gdzież są tamte zdroje,
A z nimi tyle szczęścia, nadziei tak wiele?
Kędy jest miłe latek dziecinnych wesele?

Gdzie milsze burzliwego wieku niepokoje?
Kędy jest Laura moja, gdzie są przyjaciele?
Wszystko przeszło, a czemuż nie przejdą łzy moje!

VIII
TO THE RIVER NIEMEN

Niemen, native river! Those waters are
Where? — which once played over my infant hands?
The wild, still backwater in which I swam
Seeking coolness for my yet wilder heart?

Here Laura, prideful in her beauty's shade
Braided her shining hair, with flowers tressed;
Her painted portrait on your silver breast
I more than once with foolish tears unmade!

Niemen, native river, where are those springs,
Where is my hope and all past happiness?
Where is the gaiety of my childhood years?

The gayer restlessness a first love brings?
Where are my friends? My Laura's tenderness?
Everything's passed; everything save my tears.

IX
STRZELEC

Widziałem, jak dzień cały pośród letniej spieki
Błąkał się strzelec młody; stanął nad strumieniem,
Długo poglądał wkoło i rzecze z westchnieniem:
„Chcę ją widzieć, nim kraj ten opuszczę na wieki,

„Chcę widzieć nie widziany." Wtem leci zza rzeki
Konna łowczyni strojna Dyjany odzieniem,
Wstrzymuje konia, staje, zwraca się wejrzeniem:
Zapewne jechał za nią towarzysz daleki.

Strzelec cofnął się, zadrżał i oczy Kaima
Zataczając po drodze, gorzko się uśmiechał,
Drżącą ręką broń nabił, dąsa się i zżyma,

Odszedł nieco, jakoby swej myśli zaniechał.
Wtem dojrzał mgłę kurzawy; wzniesioną broń trzyma,
Bierze na cel, mgła bliżej—lecz nikt nie nadjechał.

IX
THE ARCHER

All day through Summer's kiln-like swelter roamed
The archer. Stopping near a rivulet,
He gazed about him long and, brooding, said
"I must see her before I quit my home,
(Unseen myself)."
                Diana-garbed, a girl
On horseback rides up from the other side,
Reins in her steed, looks back with searching eye —
Surely some fellow races after her.

The archer draws back, peels his Cain-like eyes
And scans the road, tight lips a bitter grin.
Trembling with rage, pulling the bow-string taut,

He stops — as if abandoning the thought —
Then sights a dusty mist. Again locked in
To target, aims, aims — yet no one arrives.

X
BŁOGOSŁAWIEŃSTWO
Z PETRARKI

Błogosławiony rok ów, miesiąc i niedziela,
I dzień ów, i dnia cząstka, i owa godzina,
I chwila, i to miejsce, gdzie moja dziewczyna
Uczucia mi natchnęła, choć ich nie podziela.

Błogosławione oczki blasku i wesela,
Skąd amorek wygląda i łuczek napina,
Błogosławiony łuczek, strzałki i chłopczyna,
Co do mnie wówczas strzelił, ach! i dotąd strzela.

Błogosławię ci, pierwsza piosnko nieuczona,
Którą odbiły lasy domowe i rzeki,
Którą potem ojczysta powtarzała strona.

Błogosławię ci, pióro, którym w czas daleki
Wsławiłem Ją, i moja pierś błogosławiona,
W której Laura mieszkała i mieszka i na wieki.

X
BENEDICTION
FROM PETRARCH

Blest be that year, that month, that day apart —
Blest that day's fragment, blest the hour thereof,
Blest the moment and place where first my love
Blest me with love in which She takes no part.

Blest be those flashing eyes, which bless and thrill —
Cupid's casements, through which he plies his bow;
Blest be that bow, that dart, and plump fellow
Who shot me then, and, ah! shoots at me still!

I bless you, O first untaught, love-sprung rhyme
Which home-cored woods and river first echoed,
(And later by one thousand loves was blest!)

I bless you, pen, with which I long ago
Glorified Her, and blessed be my breast
In which Laura lives and reigns for all time!

XI
REZYGNACJA

Nieszczęśliwy, kto próżno o wzajemność woła,
Nieszczęśliwszy jest, kogo próżne serce nudzi,
Lecz ten u mnie ze wszystkich nieszczęśliwszy ludzi,
Kto nie kocha, że kochał, zapomnieć nie zdoła.

Widząc jaskrawe oczy i bezwstydne czoła,
Pamiątkami zatruwa rozkosz, co go łudzi;
A jeśli wdzięk i cnota czucie w nim obudzi,
Nie śmie z przekwitłem sercem iść do stóp anioła.

Albo drugimi gardzi, albo siebie wini,
Minie ziemiankę, z drogi ustąpi bogini,
A na obiedwie patrząc żegna się z nadzieją.

I serce ma podobne do dawnej świątyni,
Spustoszałej niepogód i czasów koleją,
Gdzie bóstwo nie chce mieszkać, a ludzie nie śmieją.

XI
RESIGNATION

Unhappy he, whose love is never felt,
Unhappier he, whose void heart gathers dust,
Unhappiest he: of once-loved heart, who must
Awake each day to throbbing, ancient welts.

Moving amongst glaring eyes and haughty chins,
Memory poisons delight, which cruelly tempts;
And should some kindness move his gentler sense,
His withered heart: "And how should you begin?"

Disdaining others, or riddled with self-blame,
Passing by mortal, of goddess keeping clear,
He looks upon each with a hopeless air …

And his heart is german to an ancient fane,
Racked by the wind and rain and passing years,
In which gods scorn to live and folk don't dare.

XII
DO * * *

Patrzysz mi w oczy, wzdychasz; zgubna twa prostota!
Lękaj się jadu, który w oczach źmii płonie,
Uciekaj, nim cię oddech zatruty owionie,
Jeśli nie chcesz kląć reszty twojego żywota.

Szczerość, jeszcze mi jedna pozostała cnota;
Wiedz, że niegodny ogień zapalasz w mym łonie;
Lecz umiem żyć samotny—i po cóż przy zgonie
Ma się wikłać w me losy niewinna istota?

Lubię rozkosz, lecz zwodzić nadto jestem dumny;
Tyś dziecko, mnie namiętne przepaliły bole;
Tyś szczęśliwa, twe miejsce w biesiadników kole,

Moje, gdzie są przeszłości smętarze i trumny.
Młody bluszczu, zielone obwijaj topole,
Zostaw cierniom grobowe otaczać kolumny.

XII
TO * * *

Lost one, you sigh, and gaze into my eyes,
Which burn with viper's venom; ah, beware!
Escape, before you're ill with the foul air
That I respire, and come to curse your life.

My single virtue is sincerity:
Know that you feed in me a vulgar fire —
But I can live alone; why should this pyre
Destroy you, innocent, along with me?

I'm sensuous, but too proud for deceit.
Passion has burned me through; you, child, are good,
Happy, for laughter and for feasting born;

The graveyard of the past is my retreat.
Young ivy, wind yourself around living wood —
Leave charnel pillars to the creeping thorn!

XIII

Pierwszy raz jam niewolnik z mojej rad niewoli:
Patrzę na ciebie, z czoła nie znika pogoda;
Myślę o tobie, z myśli nie znika swoboda;
Kocham ciebie, a przecież serce mi nie boli.

Nieraz brałem za szczęście chwileczkę swawoli,
Nieraz mię obłąkała wyobraźnia młoda
Albo słówka zdradliwe i wdzięczna uroda,
Lecz wtenczas i rozkosznej złorzeczyłem doli.

Nawet owę, gdy owę kochałem niebiankę,
Ileż łez, jaki zapał, jaka niegdyś trwoga,
I żal teraz na samę imienia jej wzmiankę.

Z tobą tylko szczęśliwy, z tobą, moja droga!
Bogu chwała, że taką zdarzył mi kochankę,
I kochance, że uczy chwalić Pana Boga.

XIII

This slave's at last enraptured by his chains:
I look at you, and yet my brow's uncreased,
I think of you, and yet my mind's at peace,
I love you, yet my heart's not racked with pain.

I once considered wantonness delight;
Time was, a cunning girl might make me stray
With how she looked, or what she seemed to say;
And all the while I held her in despite.

And even while I loved Her Heavensent,
What grief and dread that ardour led me through!
(My heart's still bruised blue from those horrid days).

With you alone I've happiness — with you!
Thank God, that such a lover I've been sent!
Thank you for turning curses into praise!

XIV

*Luba! ja wzdycham, pamięć niebieskiej pieszczoty
Trują mi okropnego rozmyślania chwile.
Ach! może serce twoje, co cierpiało tyle,
Może, boję się wyrzec, pustoszą zgryzoty.*

*Luba, i cożeś winna, że twych ocząt groty
Tak palące, że usta śmieją się tak mile?
Zbyt ufałaś mej cnocie, zbyt swej własnej sile,
I nazbyt ognia Stwórca wlał w nasze istoty.*

*Przewalczyliśmy wiele i dni, i tygodni,
Młodzi, zawsze samotni, zawsze z sobą w parze,
I byliśmy oboje długo siebie godni.*

*Teraz, ach! pójdę łzami oblewać ołtarze,
Nie będę mojej żebrać przebaczenia zbrodni,
Tylko niech mię Bóg twoją zgryzotą nie karze.*

XIV

Memories of your lips, and each caress,
Poisoned by doubt, become a living hell.
Perhaps your heart, which suffered so, as well
Is writhing in remorseful bitterness?

What fault is it of yours, that your deep eyes
Burn with such flame, that your smile so enchants?
My "honour's sense," your "strength of will." What chance
Had these against our natures' checkless drives?

We fought through many days — or many years —
Young, lonely, yet together all the time;
Long were we worthy of such intercourse.

Now, I creep to bathe the altar in tears:
I won't beg God to forgive me my crime —
But spare me, he must spare me your remorse!

XV
DZIEŃDOBRY

Dzieńdobry! nie śmiem budzić, o wdzięczny widoku!
Jej duch na poły w rajskie wzleciał okolice,
Na poły został boskie ożywiając lice,
Jak słońce na pół w niebie, pół w srebrnym obłoku.

Dzieńdobry! już westchnęła, błysnął promyk w oku,
Dzieńdobry! już obraża światłość twe źrenice,
Naprzykrzają się ustom muchy swawolnice,
Dzieńdobry! słońce w oknach, ja przy twoim boku.

Niosłem słodszy dzieńdobry, lecz twe senne wdzięki
Odebrały mi śmiałość; niech się wprzódy dowiem:
Z łaskawym wstajesz sercem? z orzeźwionym zdrowiem?

Dzieńdobry! nie pozwalasz ucałować ręki?
Każesz odejść, odchodzę: oto masz sukienki,
Ubierz się i wyjdź prędko — dzieńdobry ci powiem.

XV
GOOD MORNING

Good Morning! Wait… Hush! What a gorgeous sight!
How like the sun, in morning's mist half-dressed,
Her soul — colouring cheek and swelling breast,
Yet soaring still through the sky in heavenly flight!

Good Morning! Ah! you yawn, flick tired eyes,
Good Morning! Does the light annoy you so?
Good Morning! Wanton flies sport on your nose!
Good Morning! Greet the sun, the flies, and I.

I wished you sweet "Good Morning," but your "Thanks"
Is more fit for the flies than him you love;
How's your back? Do you love me? Stop yawning!

Give me your hand. Don't look so bored and blank.
Get out? I'm going — there's no need to shove —
Get dressed and come out quickly! Good Morning!

XVI
DOBRANOC

Dobranoc! już dziś więcej nie będziem bawili,
Niech snu anioł modrymi skrzydły cię otoczy,
Dobranoc! niech odpoczną po łzach twoje oczy,
Dobranoc! niech się serce pokojem zasili.

Dobranoc! z każdej ze mną przemówionej chwili
Niech zostanie dźwięk jakiś cichy i uroczy,
Niechaj gra w twoim uchu, a gdy myśl zamroczy,
Niech się mój obraz sennym źrenicom przymili.

Dobranoc! obróć jeszcze raz na mnie oczęta,
Pozwól lica. — Dobranoc! — Chcesz na sługi klasnąć?
Daj mi pierś ucałować. — Dobranoc! zapięta.

— Dobranoc! już uciekłaś i drzwi chcesz zatrzasnąć.
Dobranoc ci przez klamkę — niestety! zamknięta!
Powtarzając: dobranoc! nie dałbym ci zasnąć.

XVI
GOOD NIGHT

Good night! Today's sweet hour already passed,
Let sleep enfold you in her dark blue wings.
Good night to eyes exhausted with weeping,
Good night! May peace refresh your heart at last.

Good night, Love! May some quiet memory —
Echo of our night's chat remain with you,
Sing you asleep, and when your sleepy, blue
Thoughts fade… then fill your dreams with me.

Good night, then. Look on me, O, just once more!
And now, your cheek… as a "good night!" The maid?
Your breast instead! Ha! Buttoned to the chin!

Good night! You slam the door. All right, you win,
Good night through the key-hole! (It's locked, of course).
Good night! Through the long hours, a serenade!

XVII
DOBRYWIECZÓR

Dobrywieczór! on dla mnie najsłodszym życzeniem;
Nigdy, czy to przed nocą dzieli nas zapora,
Czyli mię ranna znowu przywołuje pora,
Nie żegnam się, ni witam z takim zachwyceniem,

Jak w tę chwilę, wieczornym ośmielony cieniem;
Ty nawet, milczeć rada i płonić się skora,
Gdy usłyszysz życzenie dobrego wieczora,
Żywszym okiem, głośniejszym rozmawiasz westchnieniem.

Niechaj dzieńdobry wschodzi tym, co społem żyją,
Objaśniać pracę, która ich ręce jednoczy;
Dobranoc niech szczęśliwych kochanków otoczy,

Gdy z rozkoszy kielicha trosk osłodę piją;
A tym, co się kochają i swą miłość kryją,
Dobrywieczór niech przyćmi zbyt wymowne oczy.

XVII
GOOD EVENING

"Good evening!" Greeting sweetest to my ear.
Never, nor at the checkpoint of the night,
Nor when I'm summoned by the dawning light
Bid I farewell nor greet I with such cheer

As then, emboldened by the evening's shades.
Even you, with a ready blush, calm and still,
When greeted with a soft "good evening" will,
Enlivened, speak with a more cheerful grace.

"Good morning" cheers the lucky wedded pair —
Makes bright the daily toil of coupled hands;
"Good night" 's the watchword of happy amants,

When from love's soothing cup they sip delight;
For those who love, yet loving, do not dare
Avow, "Good evening" dims too-telling eyes.

XVIII
DO D.D.
WIZYTA

Ledwie wnijdę, słów kilka przemówię z nią samą:
Jużci dzwonek przeraża, wpada galonowy,
Za nim wizyta, za nią ukłony, rozmowy,
Ledwie wizyta z bramy, już druga za bramą.

Gdybym mógł, progi wilczą otoczyłbym jamą,
Stawiłbym lisie pastki, kolczate okowy,
A jeśli nie dość bronią, uciec bym gotowy
Na tamten świat, stygową zasłonić się tamą.

O przeklęty nudziarzu! ja liczę minuty,
Jak zbrodniarz, co go czeka ostatnia katusza:
Ty pleciesz błahe dzieje wczorajszej reduty.

Już bierzesz rękawiczki, szukasz kapelusza,
Teraz odetchnę nieco, wstąpi we mnie dusza…
O bogi! znowu siada, siedzi jak przykuty!

XVIII
TO D.D.
A VISIT

"Alone, at last!" is barely off my tongue
When shrieks the hateful doorbell and some fool
Pops in to bow and sit and snort and drool;
His seat's yet cool: "Madame…" another one!

Would I could ring her porch with rabid dogs,
Bear traps, or (at least) rat-poison their wine —
Or if that can't deter those social kine,
Escape with her beyond the Stygian fogs!

Brainless, blabbing sot! The minutes creep
Like graveworms over my flesh as you repeat
More numbing tidbits of that damned masqued ball…

But wait! — "My hat" (I'm startled from half-sleep)
He's leaving? Am I breathing after all?
O, God! Again he sits, screwed to the seat!

XIX
DO WIZYTUJĄCYCH

Pragniesz miłym być gościem, czytaj rady moje:
Nie dość wszedłszy donosić, o czym wszyscy wiedzą,
Że dzisiaj tam walcują, ówdzie obiad jedzą,
Zboże tanie, deszcz pada, w Grecyi rozboje.

Jeśli w salonie znajdziesz bawiących się dwoje,
Zważaj, czy cię z ukłonem, z rozmową uprzedzą,
Czyli daleko jedno od drugiego siedzą,
Czy wszystko jest na miejscu, czy w porządku stroje.

Jeśli pani co wyraz zaśmiać się gotowa,
Choć usta śmiać się nie chcą; jeśli panicz z boku
Pogląda i zegarek dobywa i chowa,

I grzeczność ma na ustach, a coś złego w oku:
Wiesz, jak ich trzeba witać? — Bywaj zdrów, bądź zdrowa.
A kiedy ich masz znowu odwiedzić? — Po roku.

XIX
TO VISITORS

A Concise Etiquette for Polite Guests:
"It's not enough to hand round worn-out news —
Waltz schedules, dinner plans, a river-cruise,
Corn prices, Greek uprisings, and the rest;

"Finding a happy pair in a salon,
Mark if they greet you, are the first to speak,
Or sit at either end of the settee;
Note well the state of the clothes they've got on,

"If Madame's ready with a happy smile
At each quip (though her humour's far from gay);
If the young man checks the time all the while

"With mien correct and curses in his eye;
How should one greet them? *Hullo, folks! Goodbye!*
And when revisit them? — Give it a year."

XX
POŻEGNANIE
DO D.D.

Odpychasz mię? — czym twoje serce już postradał?
Lecz jam go nigdy nie miał; — czyli broni cnota?
Lecz ty pieścisz innego; — czy że nie dam złota?
Lecz jam go wprzódy nie dał, a ciebie posiadał.

I nie darmo; choć skarbów przed tobąm nie składał,
Ale mi drogo każda kupiona pieszczota,
Na wagę duszy mojej, pokojem żywota;
Dlaczegoż mię odpychasz? — nadaremniem badał.

Dziś odkrywam łakomstwo nowe w sercu twojem:
Pochwalnych wierszy chciałaś; marny pochwał dymie!
Dla nich więc igrasz z bliźnich szczęściem i pokojem?

Nie kupić Muzy! W każdym ślizgałem się rymie,
Gdym szedł na Parnas z lauru wieńczyć cię zawojem,
I ten wiersz wraz mi stwardniał, żem wspomniał twe imię.

XX
FAREWELL
To D.D.

You push me back — I've lost your heart so soon?
It was never mine — you guard your honour then?
Yet pet another — for gold have a yen?
I'd ne'er a farthing, yet still I possessed you.

And that not cheaply. Though I've never lain
Treasures at your feet, each caress was bought
At a dear price — my nerves are all but shot.
You pass me by? — I'm losing sleep in vain…

Today your craving is at last revealed:
You wanted sonnets! Paltry smoke of praise!
For that you bled me dry — a muse's fame?

Verse isn't sold by ell! If I should steal
From Phoebus shoots to wreathe your head in bays
The withered leaves would crown but my own shame!

XXI
DANAIDY

Płci piękna! gdzie wiek złoty, gdy za polne kwiaty,
Za haftowane kłosem majowe sukienki,
Kupowano panieńskie serduszka i wdzięki,
Gdy do lubej gołębia posyłano w swaty?

Dzisiaj wieki są tańsze, a droższe zapłaty.
Ta, której złoto daję, prosi o piosenki;
Ta, której serce daję, żądała mej ręki;
Ta, którą opiewałem, pyta, czym bogaty.

Danaidy! rzucałem w bezdeń waszej chęci
Dary, pieśni i we łzach roztopioną duszę;
Dziś z hojnego jam skąpy, z czułego szyderca.

A choć mię dotąd jeszcze nadobna twarz nęci,
Choć jeszcze was opiewać i obdarzać muszę,
Lecz dawniej wszystko dałbym, dziś wszystko — prócz serca.

XXI
DANAÏDS

Fair sex! What happened to the Golden Age,
When one could buy a maiden's heart for less
Than wildflowers, or an embroidered dress?
When none used price-tags as a passion's gauge?

Our age is cheaper, yet the prices shock:
She, given gold, instead a song demands;
She, given my heart, desires a wedding band;
She, whom I shrine in song, asks if I've stock!

Danaïds! Into the unsounded pit
Of your desire I've thrown gift, song, and soul;
Today the wastrel into a miser turns:

And though a votive light will ever burn
In me to woman's beauty, the pocket
In which I keep my heart has no more holes.

XXII
EKSKUZA

Nuciłem o miłostkach w rówienników tłumie;
Jedni mię pochwalili, a drudzy szeptali:
„Ten wieszcz kocha się tylko, męczy się i żali,
Nic innego nie czuje lub śpiewać nie umie.

„W dojrzalsze wchodząc lata, przy starszym rozumie,
Czemu serce płomykiem tak dziecinnym pali?
Czyliż mu na to wieszczy głos bogowie dali,
Aby o sobie tylko w każdej nucił dumie?"

Wielkomyślna przestroga! — wnet z górnymi duchy
Alcejski chwytam bardon, i strojem Ursyna
Ledwiem zaczął przegrywać, aż cała drużyna

Rozpierzchła się unosząc zadziwione słuchy;
Zrywam struny i w Letę ciskam bardon głuchy.
Taki wieszcz jaki słuchacz.

XXII
APOLOGIA

I sang of love before a group of peers:
And heard some praise me, heard some whispering
"The poor, love-smitten bard! Can he but sing
Of petting, sighs, and pain through maudlin tears?

"He's shaving-age — what's with the high-school moans?
Love's crimson glow—our trembling lips — my God!
The gift of tongues bestowed on such a sod
To glorify himself in every poem?"

O blest rebuke! When, on Olympus top,
With Alkaios' lyre, in Ursyn's bardic wraps,
I cleared my throat and "Canto"ed, the whole mob

Left, shaking their heads. One by one, I snapt
The strings, flung the scrap into the Lethe.
Each pig his pearl.

Adam Mickiewicz

Sonety Krymskie / The Crimean Sonnets

Towarzyszom
Podróży krymskiej
Autor

To the Companions
of my Crimean Voyage
A.M.

Wer den Dichter will verstehen,
Muß in Dichters Lande gehen.

He who will the Poet understand
Must take himself into the Poet's land.
—Goethe, im Chuld Nameh.

I
STEPY AKERMAŃSKIE

Wpłynąłem na suchego przestwór oceanu,
Wóz nurza się w zielonność i jak łódka brodzi;
Śród fali łąk szumiących, śród kwiatów powodzi,
Omijam koralowe ostrowy burzanu.

Już mrok zapada, nigdzie drogi ni kurhanu;
Patrzę w niebo, gwiazd szukam, przewodniczek łodzi;
Tam z dala błyszczy obłok? tam jutrzenka wschodzi?
To błyszczy Dniestr, to weszła lampa Akermanu.

Stójmy! — jak cicho! — słyszę ciągnące żurawie,
Których by nie dościgły źrenice sokoła;
Słyszę, kędy się motyl kołysa na trawie,

Kędy wąż śliską piersią dotyka się zioła.
W takiej ciszy! — tak ucho natężam ciekawie,
Że słyszałbym głos z Litwy. — Jedźmy, nikt nie woła.

I
THE AKERMAN STEPPES

Putting out onto a dry ocean's endlessness,
My cart bows to the verdure, majestically rides
Amidst sighing flowers on the wavy meadows' tide,
Skirting brilliant coral holms of blooming bent grass.

Soon night overcomes us, concealing barrow and road;
I look to the heavens — seek the stars — sailors' guides…
There, far-away clouds gleam? There Lucifer rises?
That? — the Dniestr. There? — That's Akerman's lamp aglow.

But wait! — How still! — I can hear the cranes' flight
Which the eye of a falcon could not overtake;
Hear the butterfly's foot on the swaying grass fall;

Hear herbage folded back by the breast of a snake.
In such perfect silence! — My ear strains so, I might
Hear a voice from my homeland…
                              Come on.
                                    No one calls.

II
CISZA MORSKA
NA WYSOKOŚCI TARKANKUT

Już wstążkę pawilonu wiatr zaledwie muśnie,
Cichymi gra piersiami rozjaśniona woda;
Jak marząca o szczęściu narzeczona młoda
Zbudzi się, aby westchnąć, i wnet znowu uśnie.

Żagle, na kształt chorągwi gdy wojnę skończono,
Drzemią na masztach nagich; okręt lekkim ruchem
Kołysa się, jak gdyby przykuty łańcuchem;
Majtek wytchnął, podróżne rozśmiało się grono.

O morze! pośród twoich wesołych żyjątek
Jest polip, co śpi na dnie, gdy się niebo chmurzy,
A na ciszę długimi wywija ramiony.

O myśli! w twojej głębi jest hydra pamiątek,
Co śpi wpośród złych losów i namiętnej burzy;
A gdy serce spokojne, zatapia w nim szpony.

II
STILL
NEAR TARKHANKUT

The wind hardly budges the ship's ensign.
The sunlit ocean gently fills her breasts —
Like a new-betrothed girl, dreaming of happiness,
She wakes to sigh, then falls asleep again.

Sails, like flags at bled-white war's demise,
Drowse on the naked masts; the ship lightly
Rocks, as if its anchor-chain were slightly
Tugged.
        Deck-strollers laugh; a matelot sighs…

O Sea! Amid your tame animalcules
The Great Squid sleeps when moiling skies are grey;
When weather stills, he flares his fearful arms —

Like to the hydra of my memory:
Slumbering through ill-hapchance and passion-storms,
Snatching the heart when deceptive quiet rules.

III
ŻEGLUGA

Szum większy, gęściej morskie snują się straszydła,
Majtek wbiegł na drabinę, gotujcie się, dzieci!
Wbiegł, rozciągnął się, zawisł w niewidzialnej sieci,
Jak pająk czatujący na skinienie sidła.

Wiatr! — wiatr! — dąsa się okręt, zrywa się z wędzidła,
Przewala się, nurkuje w pienistej zamieci,
Wznosi kark, zdeptał fale i skróś niebios leci,
Obłoki czołem sieka, wiatr chwyta pod skrzydła.

I mój duch masztu lotem buja śród odmętu,
Wzdyma się wyobraźnia jak warkocz tych żagli,
Mimowolny krzyk łączę z wesołym orszakiem;

Wyciągam ręce, padam na piersi okrętu,
Zdaje się, że pierś moja do pędu go nagli:
Lekko mi! rzeźwo! lubo! wiem, co to być ptakiem.

III
SAILING

More fiercely wails the rushing, peopled air:
"She's up, me boys!" a sailor, laughing, climbs
Up, stretches out on invisible lines —
A spider in his touch-sensitive snare.

And, Wind! — The ship bows, breaks loose from her reins,
Pitches, dives into the chaotic sea
And, righting herself, treads the waves beneath
Her, catching the wind with her strong, sure wings.

And my soul mast-like through the tumult flies;
My mind swells out as braided sails unfurl.
Laughing, drunk with this novel gracefulness,

I fall enraptured to the clipper's breast
As if my heartbeat urged the manic hurl.

Thus then the birds, which cleave the chilly skies.

IV
BURZA

Zdarto żagle, ster prysnął, ryk wód, szum zawiei,
Głosy trwożnej gromady, pomp złowieszcze jęki,
Ostatnie liny majtkom wyrwały się z ręki,
Słońce krwawo zachodzi, z nim reszta nadziei.

Wicher z tryumfem zawył, a na mokre góry,
Wznoszące się piętrami z morskiego odmętu,
Wstąpił genijusz śmierci i szedł do okrętu,
Jak żołnierz szturmujący w połamane mury.

Ci leżą na pół martwi, ów załamał dłonie,
Ten w objęcia przyjaciół żegnając się pada,
Ci modlą się przed śmiercią, aby śmierć odegnać.

Jeden podróżny siedział w milczeniu na stronie
I pomyślił: szczęśliwy, kto siły postrada,
Albo modlić się umie, lub ma z kim się żegnać.

IV
STORM

Sails, rudder blasted, roaring flood, blizzard's howl;
The moans of the frightened; the pumps' funeste rasp;
The last line wriggles sea-ward from the sailor's grasp;
The bloody sun wests, drawing gasping Hope down.

The gale shrieks "Submit!" while the Conqueror's foot falls
On mountains of water tiered from the black sea's depths —
Thus ascends to his spoils the Genius of Death
Like a trooper kickstepping over crumbledown walls.

Some half-dead ones cower; one prayer-knots his fists;
That one kisses his friends and falls, hoping in Christ;
These kneel before Death, and pray, to drive Death back.

Amid the chaos, one voyager is silent — he sits
And reflects: Happy, he who strength in crises lacks:
Whether he prays or hugs, someone hears his goodbyes.

V
WIDOK GÓR ZE STEPÓW KOZŁOWA
PIELGRZYM I MIRZA

PIELGRZYM
Tam? czy Allah postawił ścianą morze lodu?
Czy aniołom tron odlał z zamrożonej chmury?
Czy Diwy z ćwierci lądu dźwignęli te mury,
Aby gwiazd karawanę nie puszczać ze wschodu?

Na szczycie jaka łuna! pożar Carogrodu!
Czy Allah, gdy noc chylat rozciągnęła bury,
Dla światów żeglujących po morzu natury
Tę latarnię zawiesił śród niebios obwodu?

MIRZA
Tam? — Byłem; zima siedzi, tam dzioby potoków
I gardła rzek widziałem pijące z jej gniazda.
Tchnąłem, z ust mych śnieg leciał; pomykałem kroków,

Gdzie orły dróg nie wiedzą, kończy się chmur jazda,
Minąłem grom drzemiący w kolebce z obłoków,
Aż tam, gdzie nad mój turban była tylko gwiazda.
To Czatyrdah!

PIELGRZYM
Aa!!

V
A VIEW OF MOUNTAINS FROM THE KOZLOV STEPPES
PILGRIM AND MIRZA

PILGRIM
There? Did Allah mould a wall from ice of the seas?
Did he cast angels' thrones from the frozen sky's mists?
Divon summoned to erect those vast clerestories
To block the Star-Caravan's entry from the East?

A summit of light! Inferno of Tsarograd!
Did Allah suspend that lantern among the stars
To aid the massive, ever-sailing astral cars
When the night first wrapt the earth in her dun hi'lat?

MIRZA
There? — I was. Winter sits. I saw the beaks of streams
And throats of rivers drinking from their frosty source.
Snow flew from my mouth; from my own footprints I beamed

Where eagles know no road; where the clouds end their course;
Past cradles of brume where the slumbering thunder dreams
Till, above my turban, but one sole star gleamed forth.
That's Chatyrdah!

PILGRIM
Aa!!

VI
BAKCZYSARAJ

Jeszcze wielka, już pusta Girajów dziedzina!
Zmiatane czołem baszów ganki i przedsienia,
Sofy, trony potęgi, miłości schronienia
Przeskakuje sarańcza, obwija gadzina.

Skróś okien różnofarbnych powoju roślina,
Wdzierając się na głuche ściany i sklepienia,
Zajmuje dzieło ludzi w imię przyrodzenia
I pisze Balsazara głoskami „RUINA."

W środku sali wycięta z marmuru naczynie;
To fontanna haremu, dotąd stoi cało
I perłowe łzy sącząc woła przez pustynie:

„Gdzież jesteś, o miłości, potęgo i chwało?
Wy macie trwać na wieki, źródło szybko płynie.
O hańbo! wyście przeszły, a źródło zostało."

VI
BAKCHYSARAI

Still great, now empty seat of Tatar might!
Porches and floors once brushed by pashas' brows,
Harems, baths, chambers of state, are now
But locust pits where chitin guards its right.

Through varicoloured windows enters in
Bindweed, scaling dumb wall and portal frame
To seize Belshazzar's pride in Nature's name;
The repossession writ large in dust:
                              RUIN.

In this room's centre a marble vessel stands —
The harem fountain, spared by savage time,
Its pearly tears an ageless, endless plaint:

"Where now, O praise and love and sway of Man?
Your boast of lasting rule? Springs quickly dry —
For shame! The Empires fall, the Spring remains!

VII
BAKCZYSARAJ W NOCY

Rozchodzą się z dżamidów pobożni mieszkańce,
Odgłos izanu w cichym gubi się wieczorze,
Zawstydziło się licem rubinowym zorze,
Srebrny król nocy dąży spocząć przy kochance.

Błyszczą w haremie niebios wieczne gwiazd kagańce,
Śród nich po safirowym żegluje przestworze
Jeden obłok, jak senny łabędź na jeziorze,
Pierś ma białą, a złotem malowane krańce.

Tu cień pada z menaru i wierzchu cyprysa,
Dalej czernią się kołem olbrzymy granitu,
Jak szatany siedzące w dywanie Eblisa

Pod namiotem ciemności; niekiedy z ich szczytu
Budzi się błyskawica i pędem farysa
Przelatuje milczące pustynie błękitu.

VII
BAKCHYSARAI AT NIGHT

The pious stroll out of the jammids, while over
The sleepy city the echoing izan dies;
Dusk, with her blushing cheek, colours the western skies
Before the silver king of night, her lord, her lover.

In Heaven's harem the eternal cressets swim;
Among them on the sapphire eternity steers
One cloud, like a drowsy swan on a lonely mere —
Its bosom whitefeathered, its edges gold-enlimned.

Here shadows fall from cypress-top and minaret;
Further on looms black a coven of giant stones
Like satans reclining on Eblis's carpet

Beneath night's canopy; now and then from these thrones
Lightning wakes — with the rush of a farys, it plummets
Through the desert of sapphire — swift, silent, alone.

VIII
GRÓB POTOCKIEJ

W kraju wiosny, pomiędzy rozkosznymi sady,
Uwiędłaś, młodo różo! bo przeszłości chwile,
Ulatując od ciebie jak złote motyle,
Rzuciły w głębi serca pamiątek owady.

Tam na północ ku Polsce świecą gwiazd gromady,
Dlaczegoż na tej drodze błyszczy się ich tyle?
Czy wzrok twój ognia pełen, nim zgasnął w mogile,
Tam wiecznie lecąc jasne powypalał ślady?

Polko, i ja dni skończę w samotnej żałobie;
Tu niech mi garstkę ziemi dłoń przyjazna rzuci.
Podróżni często przy twym rozmawiają grobie,

I mnie wtenczas dźwięk mowy rodzinnej ocuci;
I wieszcz, samotną piosnkę dumając o tobie,
Ujrzy bliską mogiłę i dla mnie zanuci.

VIII
AT THE TOMB OF MARIA POTOCKA

A withered rose, amidst ever-blooming trees.
(On springtime's very shores by fortune cast;
Bored through by larvae of a pined-for past;
Choked white by memory's ever-tightening weeds).

Stars clustering in the North-toward-Poland skies
Stare dumbly down upon your lonely crypt —
Witnesses to the longing of one stript
From home;
           Burnt there by ever homeward-vaning eyes.

Sister! An exile's grave awaits me too —
May some kind hand toss earth upon my tomb!
Travellers often stop here, and speak of you;

I would be soothed, too, by their northern speech:
And when some poet, musing in the gloom
Sights this mound nearby, may he sing for each.

IX
MOGIŁY HAREMU
MIRZA DO PIELGRZYMA

Tu z winnicy miłości niedojrzałe grona
Wzięto na stół Allaha; tu perełki Wschodu,
Z morza uciech i szczęścia, porwała za młodu
Truna, koncha wieczności, do mrocznego łona.

Skryła je niepamięci i czasu zasłona
Nad nimi turban zimny błyszczy śród ogrodu,
Jak buńczuk wojska cieniów, i ledwie u spodu
Zostały dłonią giaura wyryte imiona.

O wy, róże edeńskie! u czystości stoku
Odkwitnęły dni wasze pod wstydu liściami,
Na wieki zatajone niewiernemu oku.

Teraz grób wasz spójrzenie cudzoziemca plami,
Pozwalam mu, — darujesz, o wielki Proroku!
On jeden z cudzoziemców poglądał ze łzami.

IX
HAREM GRAVES
MIRZA TO PILGRIM

Here crumble dry vines stripped of unripe grapes
Crushed in great Allah's press — pearls of the East
Snatched all from happy, sunlit homeland seas
For the tomb's chill treasury. Untimely rape!

Amidst these piles a frigid turban stands —
The bunchuk of Death's legions; at the base
Of time's stone veil, which ever shields the face,
Their names faint-chiselled by the giaour's hand.

Roses of Eden! Love's declivity
Saw you bloom forth screened by the leaves of shame —
Forever veiled from the infidel's leer;

Today his eye pollutes your cemetery —
I permit this — O Prophet, spare me the blame —
He alone of heathens looks on through tears!

X
BAJDARY

Wypuszczam na wiatr konia i nie szczędzę razów;
Lasy, doliny, głazy, w kolei, w natłoku
U nóg mych płyną, giną jak fale potoku;
Chcę odurzyć się, upić tym wirem obrazów.

A gdy śpieniony rumak nie słucha rozkazów,
Gdy świat kolory traci pod całunem mroku,
Jak w rozbitym źwierciedle, tak w mym spiekłym oku
Snują się mary lasów i dolin, i głazów.

Ziemia śpi, mnie snu nie ma; skaczę w morskie łona,
Czarny, wydęty bałwan z hukiem na brzeg dąży,
Schylam ku niemu czoło, wyciągam ramiona,

Pęka nad głową fala, chaos mię okrąży;
Czekam, aż myśl, jak łódka wirami kręcona,
Zbłąka się i na chwilę w niepamięć pogrąży.

X
BAIDARY

The mad horse dashes on with wind-whipt reins —
A blur of valleys, cliffs and dappled woods
Sails past my feet as if a surging flood
Making me drunk with a whirlwind of scenes.

And when the foam-lipped steed, exhausted, rests,
When beneath the shroud of dusk pales the still world,
The shattered mirror of my mind's aswirl
With dreams of valleys, cliffs and forests.

The land sleeps, yet I'm sleepless — to the sea
I race, where swollen breakers rush the shore,
Stretch out my arms and sea-ward hurl my brow;

The billow bursts above me. All around
Is chaos. There I roll, till memory
Is sucked down and (for a while) is no more.

XI
AŁUSZTA W DZIEŃ

Już góra z piersi mgliste otrząsa chylaty,
Rannym szumi namazem niwa złotokłosa,
Kłania się las i sypie z majowego włosa,
Jak z różańca kalifów, rubin i granaty.

Łąka w kwiatach, nad łąką latające kwiaty,
Motyle różnofarbne, niby tęczy kosa,
Baldakimem z brylantów okryły niebiosa;
Dalej sarańcza ciągnie swój całun skrzydlaty.

A kędy w wodach skała przegląda się łysa,
Wre morze i odparte z nowym szturmem pędzi;
W jego szumach gra światło jak w oczach tygrysa,

Sroższą zwiastując burzę dla ziemskiej krawędzi;
A na głębinie fala lekko się kołysa
I kąpią się w niej floty i stada łabędzi.

XI
ALUSHTA BY DAYLIGHT

The mountain shrugs off its misty hi'lat:
The bobbing corn whispers its morning prayer.
The forest bows and spills from May-fresh hair
Decades of mulberries and pomegranates.

Above the flowered meadow flowers crowd
In hosts of papillons — a rainbow's scythe —
A baldachin of gems to shade the skies!
Nearby the locust drags his winged shroud.

And where the stoic cliff ponders the tide,
The waves, repulsed, just storm again in rage
To charge the shore anew. Reflected light

Darts from the surge as from a tiger's eyes
And further out, where gently swells the riding billow, sun-basking flocks of swans bathe.

XII
AŁUSZTA W NOCY

Rzeźwią się wiatry, dzienna wolnieje posucha,
Na barki Czatyrdahu spada lampa światów,
Rozbija się, rozlewa strumienie szkarłatów
I gaśnie. Błędny pielgrzym ogląda się, słucha:

Już góry poczerniały, w dolinach noc głucha,
Źródła szemrzą jak przez sen na łożu z bławatów;
Powietrze tchnące wonią, tą muzyką kwiatów,
Mówi do serca głosem tajemnym dla ucha.

Usypiam pod skrzydłami ciszy i ciemnoty;
Wtem budzą mię rażące meteoru błyski,
Niebo, ziemię i góry oblał potop złoty!

Nocy wschodnia! ty na kształt wschodniej odaliski
Pieszczotami usypiasz, a kiedym snu bliski,
Ty iskrą oka znowu budzisz do pieszczoty.

XII
ALUSHTA AT NIGHT

Brisk winds revive as day's long swelter ends.
The world's lamp on Chatyrdah's shoulder falls,
Breaks open, pours liquid fire over all,
And dies. The errant pilgrim's ear attends:

Black mountain peaks, deaf valleys all around,
Springs mutter through their sleep on silken beds;
The delicate music of violets —
Hymned of uncanny, solely-heartfelt sounds.

I drowse beneath the still wings of darkness…
A meteor's dazzling flash jolts open my eye —
Earth, Mountains, Sky in living gold are steeped!

Oh odalisque! Sweet oriental Night!
You stroke aslumber, yet when I'm near sleep,
Flashing your eye, wake me to fresh caress!

XIII
CZATYRDAH

MIRZA

Drżąc muślemin całuje stopy twej opoki
Maszcie krymskiego statku, wielki Czatyrdahu!
O minarecie świata! o gór padyszachu!
Ty, nad skały poziomu uciekłszy w obłoki,

Siedzisz sobie pod bramą niebios, jak wysoki
Gabryjel pilnujący edeńskiego gmachu.
Ciemny las twoim płaszczem, a janczary strachu
Twój turban z chmur haftują błyskawic potoki.

Nam czy słońce dopieka, czyli mgła ocienia,
Czy sarańcza plon zetnie, czy giaur pali domy —
Czatyrdahu, ty zawsze głuchy, nieruchomy,

Między światem i niebem jak drogman stworzenia,
Podesławszy pod nogi ziemie, ludzi, gromy,
Słuchasz tylko, co mówi Bóg do przyrodzenia.

XIII
CHATYRDAH

      MIRZA

Your foot the trembling Muslim stoops to kiss,
Mast of the Crimean Ark, great Chatyrdah!
World-minaret! Of mountains, Padishah!
Cloud-piercer, rising over humble cliffs,

Seated before Allah's gates like supreme
Gabriel, who guards Eden's entry-ways,
Your turban weft of cloud — Fear's janissaries
Embroider this with gold-shot lightning streams.

And whether drought or mist plague us below,
Crops locust-spoiled or cities heathen-burnt,
Chatyrdah! Ever mute, unmoved and meet,

Betwixt earth and sky, creation's translator
You stand, heedless of the worlds at your feet,
Attending God's soft teaching voice alone.

XIV
PIELGRZYM

U stóp moich kraina dostatków i krasy,
Nad głową niebo jasne, obok piękne lice;
Dlaczegoż stąd ucieka serce w okolice
Dalekie, i — niestety! jeszcze dalsze czasy?

Litwo! piały mi wdzięczniej twe szumiące lasy
Niż słowiki Bajdaru, Salhiry dziewice;
I weselszy deptałem twoje trzęsawice
Niż rubinowe morwy, złote ananasy.

Tak daleki! tak różna wabi mię ponęta!
Dlaczegoż roztargniony wzdycham bez ustanku
Do tej, którą kochałem w dni moich poranku?

Ona w lubej dziedzinie, która mi odjęta,
Gdzie jej wszystko o wiernym powiada kochanku —
Depcąc świeże me ślady czyż o mnie pamięta?

XIV
PILGRIM

A pleasure-world, a besting-Eden clime;
Clear skies, and next me beautiful faces —
Why does my daft heart escape to places
Distant, and — alas! more distant times?

Litwa! your forests sing more gracefully
Than Salhir maid or Baidar songbird could;
I've trod with lighter heart through your black mud
Than here, through pineapples and mulberries!

So far away! and yet the pull's so strong!
Why do I, distracted, incessantly
Still sigh for that love of my dawning days?

You in the land from which I'm ripped away,
Where all speaks of a faithful love and long,
Treading in my fresh prints — Remember me?

XV
DROGA NAD PRZEPAŚCIĄ W CZUFUT-KALE
MIRZA I PIELGRZYM

MIRZA
Zmów pacierz, opuść wodze, odwróć na bok lica,
Tu jeździec końskim nogom swój rozum powierza;
Dzielny koń! patrz, jak staje, głąb okiem rozmierza,
Uklęka, brzeg wiszaru kopytem pochwyca,

I zawisnął. — Tam nie patrz! tam spadła źrenica,
Jak w studni Al-Kairu, o dno nie uderza.
I ręką tam nie wskazuj — nie masz u rąk pierza;
I myśli tam nie puszczaj, bo myśl jak kotwica,

Z łodzi drobnej ciśniona w niezmierność głębiny,
Piorunem spadnie, morza do dna nie przewierci,
I łódź z sobą przechyli w otchłanie chaosu.

PIELGRZYM
Mirzo, a ja spójrzałem! Przez świata szczeliny
Tam widziałem — com widział, opowiem — po śmierci,
Bo w żyjących języku nie ma na to głosu.

XV
PATH ON THE CHASM IN CHUFUT-KALE
MIRZA AND PILGRIM

        MIRZA
Say a prayer, drop the reigns, turn eyes aloof!
Here the smart rider trusts his horse's ways.
See him pause and measure with knowing gaze
The depth — kneel, find the path-edge with his hoof —

And hang there.
                Don't look down! The pupil drops
As in the bottomless well at Al-Kair.
Don't move. Don't even fling a thought out there,
For thought — a small boat's anchor — will not stop

Finding no sea-floor, but drag one
With it into the black, chaotic depths
Which swallow man and beast, and life, and hope.

        PILGRIM
Yet I looked into this rent in the globe!
And what I saw — I'll say — but after death —
There are no words for it in any living tongue!

XVI
GÓRA KIKINEIS

MIRZA

Spójrzyj w przepaść — niebiosa leżące na dole,
To jest morze; — śród fali zda się, że ptak-góra,
Piorunem zastrzelony, swe masztowe pióra
Roztoczył kręgiem szerszym niż tęczy półkole

I wyspą śniegu nakrył błękitne wód pole.
Ta wyspa żeglująca w otchłani — to chmura!
Z jej piersi na pół świata spada noc ponura;
Czy widzisz płomienistą wstążkę na jej czole?

To jest piorun! — Lecz stójmy, otchłanie pod nogą,
Musim wąwóz przesadzić w całym konia pędzie;
Ja skaczę, ty z gotowym biczem i ostrogą,

Gdy zniknę z oczu, patrzaj w owe skał krawędzie:
Jeśli tam pióro błyśnie, to mój kołpak będzie;
Jeżeli nie, już ludziom nie jechać tą drogą.

XVI
THE MOUNTAIN KIKINEIS

MIRZA
Look into the abyss. The blue below
There is the sea — Bird-Mountain, it seems,
Lies dead upon the waves; his massive wings
Forming an arc wider than a rainbow.

This chasm-spanning titan is a cloud!
A snow-thick island sailing on the blue,
Shrouding half the world in night-like gloom.
You see the flaming ribbon on its brow?

A lightning bolt! But wait here at the edge —
We must leap across the gorge at full gallop.
I'm first — be ready with your whip and goad —

When you lose me from sight, look to that ledge:
You see a feather shine there — that's my cap.
You don't — no other mortal takes this road.

XVII
RUINY ZAMKU W BAŁAKŁAWIE

Te zamki, połamane w zwaliska bez ładu,
Zdobiły cię i strzegły, o niewdzięczny Krymie!
Dzisiaj sterczą na górach jak czaszki olbrzymie,
W nich gad mieszka lub człowiek podlejszy od gadu.

Szczeblujmy na wieżycę, szukam herbów śladu;
Jest i napis, tu może bohatera imię,
Co było wojsk postrachem, w zapomnieniu drzymie,
Obwinione jak robak liściem winogradu.

Tu Grek dłutował w murach ateńskie ozdoby,
Stąd Italczyk Mongołom narzucał żelaza
I mekkański przybylec nucił pieśń namaza.

Dziś sępy czarnym skrzydłem oblatują groby,
Jak w mieście, które całkiem wybije zaraza,
Wiecznie z baszt powiewają chorągwie żałoby.

XVII
CASTLE RUINS IN BALAKLAVA

These strongholds, crumbled into shapeless heaps
Were once your pride and safeguard, thankless land!
Today like brittle skulls of giants they stand —
Where only reptile, or man still viler, creeps.

Let's climb the turret — here's some heraldries —
Faint scratchings: perhaps some bloodcurdling name —
Perhaps some hero unspilt to by fame,
Forgotten, like a slug hid in grape leaves.

Here are Greek friezes cut into the stone;
From here Latins flung iron at Mongol troops;
Here the Muslim arrival namaza intoned.

Today but black-winged vultures wheel about the graves,
Black as the mourning flags which sadly droop
From each home in a town broken by plague.

XVIII
AJUDAH

Lubię poglądać wsparty na Judahu skale,
Jak śpienione bałwany to w czarne szeregi
Ścisnąwszy się buchają, to jak srebrne śniegi
W milijonowych tęczach kołują wspaniale.

Trącą się o mieliznę, rozbiją na fale,
Jak wojsko wielorybów zalegając brzegi,
Zdobędą ląd w tryumfie i na powrót zbiegi,
Miecą za sobą muszle, perły i korale.

Podobnie na twe serce, o poeto młody!
Namiętność często groźne wzburza niepogody,
Lecz gdy podniesiesz bardon, ona bez twej szkody

Ucieka w zapomnienia pogrążyć się toni
I nieśmiertelne pieśni za sobą uroni,
Z których wieki uplotą ozdobę twych skroni.

XVIII
AJUDAH

It's pleasant to look on from Judah-side
As foaming breakers in their ebon rows
Fold rank, then gush forth spume like silver snows
And wheeling irised hosts born of the tide,

Smashed by the surf, spun round in swarthy whorls.
The waves, like troops of whales storm the cape,
Conquer in triumph, then backward escape
Leaving behind a hoard of pearls and corals.

Such is it with your own heart, Poet young!
In passion's flood engulfed when Heaven lours,
Yet just pick up your lyre —
                             the waves recede,
Ebbing away into oblivion,
And songs immortal strewing on the beach —
From which Time twines the laurels for your brow.

Uncollected Sonnets

PRZYPOMNIENIE
SONET

Lauro! czyliż te piękne wieków naszych lata,
Jeszcze się kiedy twojej malują pamięci?
Kiedyśmy sami tylko i sobą zajęci,
Dbać nie chcieli o resztę obcego nam świata.

Chłodnik, co się zielonym jaźminem wyplata,
Strumień, co z miłym szmerem po łące się kręci;
Tam nas często, wzajemne tłumaczących chęci,
Późnej nocy miłośna osłoniła szata.

A księżyc spod bladego wyjrzawszy obłoku,
Śnieżne piersi i złote rozświecał pierścienie,
Boskiego wdziękom twoim przydając uroku.

Wtenczas serca porywa słodkie zachwycenie,
Usta się spotykają, oko ginie w oku,
Łza ze łzą, i z westchnieniem miesza się westchnienie!

1818

A REMINDER
SONNET

Those glorious summers, Laura, our delight —
They've not, completely, from your memory flown?
When we, concerned with us, and us alone,
Cared not a fig for the strange world outside?

The cool larder, where the green jasmine winds,
The stream that glides by with soft, plaintive moan,
There often we, by the same yearning drawn
Did bear our hearts, safe in night's lovely blind,

Whilst from a cloud the moon broke, pouring clear
Upon gold ring and snowy breast its light,
Adding its charms divine to your own grace.

Our hearts were ravished by a sweet delight;
Our eyes met, and our lips, as we'd embrace,
Commingling sigh with sigh, and tear with tear.

1818

[Jak wielorakie świecą na tym błoniu kwiaty!]
[W IMMIONIKU M.S.]

Jak wielorakie świecą na tym błoniu kwiaty!
Jedne szumne w jaskrawych dowcipu ozdobach,
Drugie przyjaźń sadziła; te wzrastają z laty;
Inne żałośnie więdnąć zdają się na grobach,
W których są pochowane serca i nadzieje.
Kiedy Pani przechodzi ten ogród pamiątek,
Nad jednym może westchnie, z wielu się rozśmieje,
Ujrzy i szczupły dla mnie oddany zakątek.
A choć równie z innymi nie możesz go cenić,
Chociaż wyda się tylko samotną drożyną,
Która, długiego słońca i niepogód winą,
Nie może się zakwiecić, ani zazielenić:
Wspomnisz jednak o dróżce, choć z tego powodu,
Że przedziela kwatery pięknego ogrodu.

Kowno 1824, Mca Aug. Dnia 16.

[How varied and how sweet, the blossoms that wave]
[IN M.S.'S SCRAPBOOK]

How varied, and how sweet, the blooms that wave
Above this garden! Artful some, and gay,
Some aged, earnest, others like friends at play,
Still others seem to wither on a grave
Which hides, perhaps, some broken heart, or hope.
You stroll about these beds of memory;
This flower makes you laugh, and here you mope —
And there: the patch that's been reserved for me.
It's not as lovely as the other ones:
A dusty patch it seems, overcast with gloom,
Sodden by too much rain, scorched by such suns
As never shall it glow with grass or bloom
And yet, this dry path shall not be forgot,
Because it splits in twain your garden plot.

Kowno, 16 August 1824

PCHŁA I RABIN

Pewny rabin w Talmudzie kąpiąc się po uszy,
Cierpiał, że go pchła gryzła; w końcu się obruszy:
Dalej czatować, złowił. Siedzi przyciśnięta,
Kręci się, wyciągając główkę i nożęta:
"Daruj, Rabi, mądremu nie godzi się gniewać:
Potomkowi Lewitów możnaż krew przelewać?"
"Krew za krew! — wrzasnął Rabin — Belijala płodzie!
Filistynko, na cudzej wytuczona szkodzie!
Mrówki swój mają szpichlerz; pracowite roje
Znoszą miody i woski, a trucień napoje:
Ty się jedna śród ludzi z liwarem uwijasz,
Pijaczko tym szkodliwsza, iż cudze wypijasz."
Zakończył, i gdy więźnia bez litości dłabi,
Pchła konając pisnęła: "A czym żyje rabi?"

[1825-1826]

THE FLEA AND THE RABBI

A rabbi, learned in Talmudic Writ,
By pesky flea was badgered, sucked at, bit;
At last he caught the vermin, who, distressed,
Panicked and wriggling, peeped out this request:
"Forgive me, Reb! Is it a seemly thing
For you to kill? Of Levites the offspring?"
"Blood's price is blood, Belial's filthy brat!
You Philistine! On other's juice grown fat!
Ants have their pantry; honeybee and drone
Both sweat with honest labour; you alone
Suck others' blood, you parasitic scum!"
At this, he crushed the flea beneath his thumb...
Expiring, with his ghost, these words outflew:
"In this, Reb, how'm I different from you?"

[1825-1826]

NIEZNAJOMEJ SIOSTRZE PRZYJACIÓŁKI MOJEJ

Przyjaciele, wyrokiem smutnym rozłączeni,
Kiedy im wszystko stawi na ziemi przegrody,
Wybierają spomiędzy niebieskich promieni
Wspólną gwiazdę za wiecznej powiernicę zgody,
I tą gwiazdą jak krzyżem świętego pierścienia,
Zaślubiają wzajemne przynajmniej wspomnienia.

Ale jest milsza gwiazda, która przyjaźń budzi
W sercach dwojga dalekich, nieznajomych ludzi;
Dopóki błyszczeć będzie na północnem niebie,
Patrząc ku niej, nam udziel choć cząstkę wejrzenia.

A kiedy nas opuści, by świecić dla ciebie,
Poślę za nią ku tobie oczy i życzenia.

O! gdyby dozwoliły wyroki łaskawsze
Widzieć tę gwiazdę społem i z bliska i zawsze!

W Moskwie, dnia 1 X 1827

TO MY FRIEND'S SISTER, UNMET

When friends must part, severed by unkind fate,
And everything on earth keeps them afar,
They choose, from out the fires that radiate
In the night sky, as testament, a star,
Upon which, as upon the Cross, to swear
Each other… in their memory to bear.

But there's another star, and with its rise,
Friendship is born in distant hearts, so sweet,
That while it shines aloft in Northern skies,
Gazing at it, at least our eyes might meet.

For when it sets, to shed its light on you,
I send with it my eyes and wishes true.

O! That it might our harsh fate override,
That we might view it, always, side by side!

Moscow, 1 X 1827

SONET

Rozeszliśmy się wczora weseli i zdrowi;
Wczora moją zostałaś — dziś z nowym pośpiechem,
Z nowym ogniem w źrenicach i wyższym uśmiechem
Biegłem po szczęście, które dzisiaj się odnowi.

Wzdychasz? nie chcesz pokazać oczu kochankowi?
I ma pierś mimowolnem ozwała się echem
Na ten głos niewinności przestraszonej grzechem,
I me oko musiało oddać hołd wstydowi.

Ten smutek, ten wstyd nową dla ciebie ozdobą.
Lecz jeśli się pod nimi zgryzota ukrywa
I krótką radość — wieczną chce zaćmić żałobą,

O kochanko, ich widok serce mi rozrywa.
Nie chcę więcej tych westchnień i rumieńców z tobą.
Bądź mi mniej doskonała, a więcej szczęśliwa.

SONNET

I left you last night in good spirits, and well;
You became mine at last! Now, today, with new haste,
New fire in my eye, a surer smile, I race
To rejoice in my new, hourly-doubling heart's wealth.

Yet you sigh — your eyes wander; you redden with shame.
And I must, unwillingly, homage the dim
Full-eyed paleness of innocence, frightened of sin;
Respond to the questions your sinlessness frames.

This impeccable sadness adds to your beauty.
Yet if underneath all roils the worm of remorse,
Boring through our new joy like a cold, still-born corpse,

These immaculate tears burn of acid and gall.
Dry your eyes. I will go before another fall.
Be more happy, my Love, and less perfect to me.

Gdzie dawniej źrenicami oświecane twemi
Kwiaty wschodziły godne archanielskiej skroni,
Potem rwałem ci bukiet na tej samej błoni,
Pomieszany z piołunem, z wierzby płaczącemi.

Kiedy ją chwast i blekot na zawsze zaciemi,
Żaden się czysty kwiatek na niej nie zapłoni;
I wtenczas bukiet przyjmij: nie godzien twej dłoni,
Lecz zrósł na poświęconej twym pobytem ziemi.

Ach! podobne me serce do owej krainy:
Niegdyś bliskie twych piersi, w młodzieńczej ozdobie
Niosło ci piękne czucia i szlachetne czyny.

Dziś występne, niestety, szle ze swojej winy,
Choć dla drugich w szalonej cierpiało chorobie;
Nie gardź nim! było kiedyś poświęcone tobie.

Your eyes once called to life a rich meadow
Where petals splayed worthy of angels' brows;
From there I bring you this bouquet of flowers
And willow-strands, twined with a wormwood bow.

When hemlock shades that plot and cultures weeds,
No flower will push up through the blighted land.
Even then take this straw — unworthy of your hand,
Yet sprung from soil once given you in deed.

This garden is the image of my heart:
Once near your bosom, resplendent in its youth
It bore you love, accomplishments of worth;

Now knavish, sadly — sick with sin and ruth
(As once with compassion) — don't disregard! —
You lived here once — this once was hallowed earth.

JASTRZĄB
NA WYSOKOŚCI KIKINEIS (DO*)

Biedny jastrząb, śród niebios porwała go chmura,
W obcy zaniosła żywioł i dalekie strony;
Morską presiąkły rosą, wichrami znużony,
Śród ludzi na tym maszcie roztoczył swe pióra.

Lecz go żadna bezbożna nie pochwyci ręka,
Bezpieczny, jakby siedział na leśnej gałęzi;
On jest gościem, Giovanno; kto gościa uwięzi,
Jeżeli jest na morzu, niech się burzy lęka.

Wspomni na moje, wspomni na twe własne dzieje;
I tyś na życia morzu — widziałaś straszydła,
I mnie wicher odpędził, słota zlała skrzydła.

Po cóż te słowa miłe, te zdradne nadzieje?
Sama w niebezpieczeństwie — drugim stawisz sidła.
[...]

THE HAWK
AT SEA, NEAR KIKINEIS (TO*)

Poor hawk! Teased from his home by bluffing clouds;
Soaked by sea-mist strange to his wooded pale,
Whipped round by foreign winds, the unknown gale
Set him upon this mast amidst gaping crowds.

Yet no impious hand will do him harm —
Safe he, as if on forest branch at rest.
A guest, Giovanna — he who fetters a guest
Be he on the sea — let him look out for storms.

Remember what befell both you and me —
You, sea-tossed, prey to waves and sea bugbears,
I, storm-chased, wings-wet-through, with brine well soaked.

Then why the pretty words — the treacherous hopes?
Unsafe yourself, for me you're setting snares?
[...]

SONET

Poezyjo! gdzie cudny pędzel twojej ręki?
Gdy chcę malować, za cóż myśli i natchnienia
Wyglądają z wyrazów, jak zza krat więzienia,
Kryjących i szpecących tak ubogie wdzięki?

Poezyjo! gdzie twoje melodyjne dźwięki?
Śpiewam — ona mojego nie usłyszy pienia:
Jako słowik, król śpiewu, nie słyszy strumienia,
Który w podziemnej głębi rozwodzi swe jęki.

Nie tylko dźwięk i kolor, aniołowie myśli,
Lecz i pióro, roboczy niewolnik poety,
Na cudzej [ziemi] nie zna praw dawnego pana

I zamiast pieśni, znaki niepojęte kryśli:
Muzyczne znaki pieśni… lecz ta pieśń niestety,
[Nigdy jej miłym głosem nie będzie śpiewana.]

SONNET

Euterpe! Where've you hid the magic brush?
I dab away, yet thought and sentiment
Stare out from words as if in cages pent
Which block their escape, stifling their happy rush!

Euterpe! Pipe me down some lovely tunes!
I croon, yet she can't hear the song I sing —
A nightingale, she — who hears no stream
Which far beneath the sod sobs on and moans.

Not only sound and shade, angelic thoughts,
But pen as well — the poet's tireless slave —
On foreign turf heeds not his master's will:

Instead of song, signs indecipherable
Traces — song signs — writ to be forgot —
Unsung by her, born to a bastard's grave.

DO SAMOTNOŚCI

Samotności! do ciebie biegnę jak do wody
    Z codziennych życia upałów;
Z jakąż rozkoszą padam w jasne, czyste chłody
    Twych niezgłębionych kryształów.

Nurzam się i wybijam w myślach nad myślami,
    Igram z nimi jak z falami:
Aż ostygły, znużony, złożę moje zwłoki —
    Choć na chwilę — w sen głęboki.

Tyś mój żywioł: ach, za cóż te jasnych wód szyby
    Studzą mi serce; zmysły zaciemiają mrokiem,
I za cóż znowu muszę na kształt ptaka-ryby,
    Wyrywać się w powietrze, słońca szukać okiem?

I bez oddechu w górze, bez ciepła na dole,
    Równie jestem wygnańcem w oboim żywiole!

[wiosna 1832]

TO SOLITUDE

Solitude! I rush to you, as to a pool
        From the day's scorching blight,
And as I hurl myself into your pure, cool
        Crystalline depths, O, what delight!

I plunge in thoughts, skim over them, as well,
        Playing with them, like the sea's swell
Until, cooled down, exhausted, nearly dead
        I flee care — for a while — asleep in bed.

You are my element! O, how I'd wish
        To keep my heart cool in the depths, the dark…
Why must I ever, like the flying fish
        Spurt out sunwards, like some ungainly lark?

Gasping above, and shivering in the sea,
        Exiled in both, in both a refugee.

[spring 1832]

THE POET'S CLARIFICATIONS

The Erotic Sonnets

XXII. APOLOGIA

— *With Alkaios' lyre.*
    Alkaios' lyre, or the "bardon," is a musical instrument named after the famous Greek lyric poet Alkaios (Alcaeus). Born in Mytilene, he flourished circa 600 B.C.

— *in Ursyn's bardic wraps.*
    Ursyn is the sobriquet of Julian Niemcewicz.

—*...flung the scrap into the Lethe.*
    The Lethe is the river of forgetfulness in Elysium. From it the souls of the dead were said to drink in order to forget their earthly sufferings. After several ages, when the souls were to return to life in a new incarnation, they were to drink from the river for a second time, so as to erase the secrets of the other world from their memory. (Mythological).

The Crimean Sonnets

I. THE AKERMAN STEPPES

— *Skirting brilliant coral holms of blooming bent grass.*
    "Bent grass," or *burzan*. Ukrainians, and those living in the area between the Dniester and the Boh Rivers, use this name when speaking of large bushes which, when covered with flowers in Summer, provide the steppe with a pleasant variety.

V. A VIEW OF MOUNTAINS FROM THE KOZLOV STEPPES

— *Divon summoned to erect those vast clerestories.*
　　According to ancient Persian mythology, *Divon* are malevolent genii who at one time reigned over the earth. Conquered later by the angels, they now live at the edge of the world, beyond the mountain Qaf.

— *A summit of light! Inferno of Tsarograd!*
　　For a while at sunset the peaks of Chatyrdah appear to be aflame due to a phenomenon caused by brilliantly reflected sunbeams.

— *When the night first wrapt the earth it her dun hi'lat.*
　　The *Hi'lat* is a ceremonial cloak of honour, which the sultan presents to important state officials.

— *That's Chatyrdah!*
　　The highest of the peaks in the southern Crimean range, Chatyrdah may be seen from a distance of nearly 200 versts [213.4 km; 132.6 m], from all directions, in the shape of a giant bluish cloud.

VI. BAKCHYSARAI

In a valley surrounded completely by mountains lies the city of Bakchysarai, one-time capital of the Crimean khans of the Girei dynasty.

— *To seize Belshazzar's pride in Nature's name, / The repossession writ large in dust:/* RUIN
　　"In the same hour came forth fingers of a man's hand, and wrote over against the candlestick upon the plaister of the wall of the king's palace: and the king saw the part of the hand that wrote." *The Prophecy of Daniel*, V, 25, 26, 27, 28.

VII. BAKCHYSARAI AT NIGHT

— *The pious stroll out of the jammids.*
  "Mesjids, or Jammids, are regular mosques. On the outside, at each corner of the temple a thin turret shoots up into the sky. These minarets (*menaré*) are encircled at their half-way point by a gallery (*shurfé*) from which the *muezzins* or announcers call the people to prayer. This calling-forth is known as the *izan*. Five times each day at the designated hours the *izan* is sung forth from all the minarets, and the clean, sonorous voices of the *muezzins* pleasantly resound throughout the airways of the Muslim towns in which, because of the absence of wheeled conveyance, an especial stillness prevails." (Sękowski, *Collectanea*, Vol. I f. 66).

— *Like satans reclining on Eblis's carpet.*
  Among Muslims, Lucifer is known by the names Garazel and Eblis (or Iblis).

— *…with the rush of a farys, it plummets.*
  A *farys* is a knight among the Bedouin Arabs.

VIII. AT THE TOMB OF MARIA POTOCKA

Not far from the palace of the Khans stands a mausoleum built in the eastern style and topped with a round cupola. There is a legend among the peoples of the Crimean peninsula that this monument was raised by Khan Kerim Girei in honour of a slave whom he had loved well. Muravyov-Apostol, the author of a learned and beautifully written *Travels in Crimea,* holds that this legend is lacking in factual basis, and that in reality, the mausoleum contains the ashes of a Georgian maid. It's hard to say on what facts he bases his assertion, for the objection that Tatars, in the middle of the eighteenth century, wouldn't have had an easy task in seizing captives from the house of Potocki is not fully convincing. The latest Cossack disturbances in the Ukraine, during which more than a few people were seized and sold to the neighbouring Tatars, is common knowledge. Many aristocratic houses in Poland bear the name Potocki, and thus is it is no *sine qua non* that the captive mentioned above necessarily belonged to the eminent house of the heirs of Humań, which was less susceptible to Tatar invasions and the consequences of Cossack uprisings. The local legend of the tomb in Bakchysarai was used by the gifted Russian poet Aleksandr Pushkin as the basis of his verse-tale *The Bakchysarai Fountain*.

IX. HAREM GRAVES

In a delightful garden, amidst slender poplars and mulberry trees, stand the white marble mausoleums of Khans, sultans, their wives and children; in two neighbouring sites lie tombs tumbled-about without order: at one time they were richly shaped and decorated, today naked planks and shroud-rags greet the eye.

— *Amidst these piles a frigid turban stands.*
    Above Muslim graves stand turbans carved of stone, the shape of the turban determined by the gender of the deceased.

— *Their names faint-chiselled by the giaour's hand.*
    Giaour means unbeliever. Muslims apply this term to Christians.

X. BAIDARY

This is a beautiful valley through which one usually travels on one's way to the southern coast of the Crimean peninsula.

XI. ALUSHTA BY DAYLIGHT

One of the most delightful places in all of Crimea. Northern winds are never felt in Alushta; even in November the traveller is often obliged to seek coolness in the shade of huge Italian walnut trees, which are still green at this late season.

— *The bobbing corn whispers its morning prayer.*

The *Namaz* is a Muslim prayer, which the worshipper intones while seated, bowing his forehead to the ground.

— *Decades…*
Muslims use rosaries when praying. The rosaries of eminent persons are often studded with costly jewels.

— *of [ruby] mulberries and pomegranates.*
    Pomegranate and mulberry trees, blushing with delightful fruit, are common throughout the entire southern coast of Crimea.

XIII. CHATYRDAH

— *World minaret! of mountains, Padishah!*
    Padishah is the title used by the Turkish sultan.

— *Gabriel, who guards Eden's entry-ways.*
    I employ the name Gabriel here as one universally familiar, although, according to Eastern mythology, the actual guard of Heaven is Rameh (the constellation Arcturus), one of the two great stars known as *as semekein*.

XIV. PILGRIM

—*Salhir maid.*
    The Salhir is a Crimean river, which springs near the foot of Chatyrdah.

XV. PATH OVER THE CHASM IN CHUFUT-KALE

Chufut-Kale is a hamlet situated on lofty cliffs; the houses, which stand on the very edge of the precipice, have an appearance similar to swallows' nests. The path leading to the top is troubling, hanging out over the very abyss. In the village itself house-walls are almost immediately set upon the brink of the chasm; glancing through a window, the eye loses itself in the immeasurable depths.

— Here the smart rider trusts his horse's ways.
  In difficult and dangerous passes the Crimean horse seems to possess a special instinct of caution and certainty. Before it takes a step, it hesitates with its hoof in the air, then tests each stone for its sureness and ability to bear the weight of horse and rider.

XVI. THE MOUNTAIN KIKINEIS

— *There is the sea — Bird-Mountain, it seems.*
  Bird-Mountain — an old friend from the *Arabian Nights*. It is famous in Persian mythology, and many times described by Eastern poets as the bird Simurg. "Great is he (relates Firdussi in *Shah-Name*) as a mountain, powerful as a fortress, he carries elephants in his talons." Further: "Taking notice of the knights, (Simurg) started up as a cloud from his cliff-top home and swept through the air like a hurricane, casting a shadow on the army of riders." See Hammer, *Geschichte der Redekünst Persiens*. Vienna 1818, p. 65.

—*A snow-thick island sailing on the blue.*
  When one gazes upon clouds sailing above the ocean from a vantage point on a mountain above cloud-level, it seems as if the clouds were floating on the water itself like tremendous white islands. I have experienced this interesting phenomenon from the top of Chatyrdah.

XVII. CASTLE RUINS IN BALAKLAVA

On the bay bearing this name there stands the rubble of a fortress built long ago by Greek arrivals from Miletus. Later on, the Genoese raised the fortress Cembalo on the very same spot.

TRANSLATOR'S NOTES

THE EROTIC SONNETS

MOTTO
Quand'era in parte altr'uom da quel, ch'io sono. Literally: "When I was partly a different man to that, which I am now." The fourth line of the sonnet beginning "Voi ch'ascoltate in rime sparse il suono / di quei sospiri" ("O you, who hear in these scattered verses the sound / of those sighs") of Francesco da Petrarca (1304–1374). It is the first of 366 poems, mostly, but not entirely, in sonnet form, that make up the *Canzoniere*. It is this book, more than any other, upon which Petrarch's fame rests. Although not entirely centred on his *donne ideale* Laura, the volume, which spread widely throughout Europe almost contemporaneously with the poet himself (Chaucer is already working with it in England in 1380), is the grandfather of all love sonneteering. Like many other poets, Mickiewicz addresses his love-interest in the sonnets as Laura, and many of the sonnets in the Erotic cycle are inspired, if not organically linked, to the verse of the *Canzoniere*.

I
PROSE TRANSLATION: *TO LAURA. I'd barely just caught sight of you, and already I was afire, / I searched for an old acquaintance in an eye first-met; / Whilst a reciprocal blush arose on your cheeks, / like that of a rose, whose breasts were exposed by the dawn light. // You'd barely begun your song, and already I was weeping; / your voice penetrated my heart and grasped hold of my soul; / It seemed that an angel was greeting her by name, / and the clocktower of the heavens sounded the moment of salvation. // O dear! Let your eyes not fear to admit [their truth]! / If I move you, with my glance, or with my voice: / I care not that fate and people may stand ranged against us, // that I must leave hastily, and love*

without hope! / Let an earthly vow bestow your hand on someone else, / just admit this: that God has married your soul to me!...

Mickiewicz began to study the Italian language and read the sonnets of Petrarch in the original during his sojourn on the Crimean peninsula. Five sonnets from the erotic cycle show the influence of the earlier poet on the Polish bard. "To Laura" is based on the sonnet *Erano i capi d'oro all'aura sparsi*:

> *Erano i capei d'oro a l'aura sparsi,*
> *Che'n mille dolci nodi gli avolgea,*
> *E 'l vago lume altra misura ardea*
> *Di quei begli occhi, ch'or ne son sí scarsi.*
>
> *E 'l viso di pietosi color farsi,*
> *Non so se vero o falso, mi parea.*
> *I' che l'esca amorosa al petto avea,*
> *Qual meraviglia se di subito arsi?*
>
> *Non era l'andar suo cosa mortale,*
> *Ma d'angelica forma; e le parole*
> *Sonovan altro che pur voce umana.*
>
> *Uno spirito celeste, un vivo sole*
> *Fu quel ch'i' vidi, e se non fosse or tale,*
> *Piaga per allentar d'arco non sana.*

> An aureole of flowing, golden hair —
> Thousands of jealous ringlets mobbed her brow;
> Her eyes then burnt with unmatched light, which now
> Is dearer yet for being matchless rare.
> Her godlike beauty with compassion tinged,
> Her bearing worthy of a child of light—
> What marvel if she had me at first sight,
> A woodcock straining for the ready springe?
> Her very gait betrayed her ancestry
> Celestial, not of this mud-formed sphere;
> She spoke — it was as if angels had sung!
> And seraph so she was! A living sun!

Whose gleaming, after sunset, yet shines clear —
My wounds fade not with bow-string slackening.

II
PROSE TRANSLATION: *I talk to myself, and speak confusedly in conversations with others; / my heart beats violently, I cannot control my breathing; / I feel sparks in my eyes, while my face grows pale; / more than one of the strangers [around me] inquires loudly about my health, // or whispers something about my mental state into someone's ear. / Thus I endure my daily torture. When I fall upon my bed, / in hopes of stealing a few moments [of relief] from suffering, / my heart sets alight fiery nightmares in my head. // I tear myself from my bed, I run, I learn phrases by rote / with which I am to curse your cruelty, / [they are] arranged, and forgotten, millions of times. // But when I catch sight of you, I can't understand why / but again I'm calm, cooler than a stone / just to heat up again — and keep silent as before…*

— Line 8: the adjective fiery (*ogniste*) is so placed in the phrase *Serce ogniste mary zapala* that it can modify either heart (*serce*) or nightmares (*mary*). The same form *ogniste* agrees with the singular neuter noun *serce* and the plural feminine noun *mary*. So: "my fiery heart sets alight nightmares" would also be an acceptable translation of this line.

III
PROSE TRANSLATION: *Your behaviour is unrefined, your words are simple, / neither your face nor your eye outshines those of others: / but everyone is delighted to catch sight of you, delighted to listen to you, up close. / Although you wear the clothing of a shepherdess, it's obvious that you're a queen. // Yesterday songs and loud conversation resounded; / people inquired after the names of other girls your age; / this one was pouring praise upon them, another one was tossing jokes about; / [Then] you entered, and everyone observed a sacred silence. // Thus it is at a banquet, when the singer incites the chorus to song, / when the dancers wheel about the salon in rings, / and suddenly they stand and grow silent, and everyone asks — / no one knows why they suddenly all stopped, and fell into pensiveness — / "I know why," the poet says, "an angel just*

flew by." / All of those present honoured the guest, — but not everyone recognised her.

IV

PROSE TRANSLATION: *A MEETING IN THE GROVE. "Is that you? and so late?…" "I lost my way / among the forests, by the unsure light of the moon. / Did you miss me? Do you think of me?…" "You darling ingrate! / Ask rather if I'm able to think of anything else!" / "Allow me to press your hand, to kiss your foot. You're trembling! Why?…" / I don't know. Wandering about the copse, / I'm frightened by a rustling leaf, and the cry of nocturnal birds: / Ah! we must be guilty, when we feel such dread!" // "Look in my eyes, look at my brow: with such a brow / crime is never paired; dread never has such a bold appearance. / For God's sake! Are we guilty of sitting together! // After all, I sit so far away, and I say so little / and I deal with you, my earthly angel! / As if you'd already become an angel in heaven."*

To a certain extent, the imagery contained in the sonnet "Meeting in the Grove" may have been suggested by the Petrarchan sonnet *Per mezz' i boschi inospiti e selvaggi* ["Through the midst of woods inhospitable and savage"].

V

PROSE TRANSLATION: *The prayerful prude condemns us, while the libertine laughs at us, / since although we are surrounded by lonely walls, / and although she is so young, and I am so in love / I still drop my eyes, and she weeps floods of tears. // I'm defending myself from [her] tempting allures, while she / wishes to scare off all hopes, by every now and then rattling the fetters / with which our lamentable fate has shackled our hands. / We ourselves don't know what's going on in our hearts. // Is this pain or delight? When I feel the squeeze / of your hands, when I am ravished by the flames of your lips: / Dear! can I bestow upon this, the name of suffering? // But when our cheeks are bedewed with tears, / when the remains of life arise in our sighings: / Dear: is it possible for me to call this delight?*

— Lines 5-7: The syntax of the original Polish lines is thick, confusing. Mickiewicz is perhaps mimicking the chains in which the lovers' hands are entangled. This is what the lines seem to mean: *I beat back allurements — allurements which even mock hopes of future happiness, by rattling the chains with which lamentable fate has bound our hands.*

The following sonnet may be seen as the inspiration for this sonnet:

> *S'amor non è, chè dunque è quel ch'io sento?*
> *Ma s'egli è amor, per Dio, che cosa, e quale?*
> *Se bona, ond'è l'effecto aspro mortale?*
> *Se ria, ond'è sí dolce ogni tormento?*
>
> *S'a mia voglia ardo, ond'è 'l pianto e 'l lamento?*
> *S'a mal mio grado, il lamentar che vale?*
> *O viva morte, o dilectesso male,*
> *Come puoi in me, s'io no 'l consento?*
>
> *E s'io 'l consento, a gran torto mi doglio:*
> *Fra sí contrari' venti in frale barca*
> *Mi trovo in alto mar senza governo,*
>
> *Sí lieve di saver, d'error sí carca,*
> *Ch'i' medesmo non so quel ch'io mi voglio;*
> *E tremo a mezza state, ardendo il verno.*

> If Love it's not, give it another name.
> If Love it is, what kind of love, by Christ!
> A bargain, with my sanity its price?
> A torture, bearing such delicious pain?
>
> If Hell I long for, why the gnashing teeth?
> If Hell I shun, what boots the sloppy moan?
> Sweet Death-in-Life! O Blest, Delightful Woe —
> Whence your tyrannic sway o'er one unlief?
>
> (Yet disregard these plaints if you've my will)

A frail bark, flipped by contrary winds,
I'm rudderless on vast, unfriendly seas.

I've not a hint what will become of me,
Nor what I want …
                        in Summer marrow-chilled,
'Midst Winter's chilly fogs I seethe and singe.

VI

PROSE TRANSLATION: *MORNING AND EVENING. The sun shines in the east in a wreath of fiery clouds / and in the west, the moon shrouds its pale face in gloom; / the rose turns its opened buds toward the sun, / the violet kneels, bending beneath the drops of the morning [dew]. // Laura shone out in her window. I fell to my knees on the porch; / she, stroking the plaits of her golden braids, / "Why," she said, "do you all have such sad eyes in the morning, / the moon and the violet, and you too, my lover?" // That evening, I came to enjoy a new sight: / the moon returned, his face was full and ruddy, / the violet lifted her leaves refreshed by the darkness: / again my beloved stood in the window, / in yet more beautiful clothing and with a gayer eye; / once more I fell to my knees at her feet — just as sad as in the morning.*

VII

PROSE TRANSLATION: *FROM PETRARCH. Do you wish to know what I suffer, O my contemporaries? / I'll paint it as faithfully as any pen can. / Up till now I have been chasing visions in thought, through the church of my reminiscences / and my spirit dreams of the past. // Here she was used to play, there she stood pensively, / there she covered her face with aversion, here she called me with her eye, / here she was angry, there gloomy, here again gay, / here she clothed her countenance in tenderness, and there in gravity. // There she hummed a song, here she squeezed my hand, / here she sat down, there was where we first conversed. / She ran from this place, here on the sand she traced my name, // There she said a little word, here she sighed quietly, / there she blushed — ah! among these memories / my heart is constantly stumbling about, and my thoughts err confused.*

The subtitle refers to this sonnet:

Senuccio, i' vò che sappi, in qual maniera
Tractato sono, e qual vita è la mia.
Ardomi e struggo ancor com'io solia;
Laura mi volve, e son pur quel ch'i' m'era.
Qui tutte umile, e qui la vidi altera,
Or aspra, or piana, or dispietata, or pia;

Or vestirsi onestate, or leggiadria,
Or mansueta, or disgdenosa, e fera.

Qui cantò dolcemente, e qui s'assise;
Qui si rivolse, et qui rattenne il passo;
Qui co' begli occhi mi trafisse il core:

Qui disse una parola, e qui sorrise:
Qui cangiò 'l viso. In questi pensier, lasso,
Notte, e dí tiemmi il signor nostro, Amore.

Life beats on here, Senuccio, without change.
I burn and melt as I'm accustomed to,
Laura torments me as she's wont to do,
In Love's searing forge my heart remains the same.

My Laura, though, 's a mistress of disguise:
Now sharp, now quiet; spiteful, then devout;
Dressed simply, then in rocks and gold tricked out;
Here gentle — there disdain sneers thin her eyes.

Here sweetly singing, fairest among flowers;
Here bolts away in ire — here slows her pace ...
Here slays my heart with teary, defenceless gaze,

Here smiles, here laughs away the sunlit hours,
Here with sad thoughts her flawless visage lours ...
And thus beneath Amor's yoke I spend my days.

VIII

PROSE TRANSLATION: *TO THE RIVER NIEMEN.* O Niemen, O river of my homeland! Where are the waters, / which I once cupped in my infant palm, / on which I later swam in a wild retreat / seeking coolness for my uneasy heart? // Here Laura, gazing with pride at the reflection of her beauty, / liked to braid her hair and adorn her brows with flowers. / Here I, an ardent youth, sometimes with my tears ruffled / her portrait painted upon the bosom of your silver waves. // O Niemen, O river of my homeland, where are those springs, / and with them, so much happiness, so many hopes? / Whither, the pleasant joys of my childhood years? // Where are the even more pleasant anxieties of my stormy age? // Whither my Laura, where are my friends? / Everything's passed away, but why will my tears not pass away?

IX

PROSE TRANSLATION: *THE ARCHER.* I once saw, as through an entire scorching summer day / a young archer erred; he stopped at a stream, / and for a long while looked about himself, and [then] said with a sigh: / "I want to see her [again] before I leave this land forever. // I want to see her, unseen myself." Then, from beyond the river, came flying / a huntress on horseback, dressed in the garb of Diana. / She pulled up her horse, paused, and threw a glance behind her; / certainly, a companion, from afar, was riding after her. // The archer drew back, shivered, and with the eyes of Cain, / stumbling along the path and smiling bitterly, / strung his weapon with shaking hand, pouting and flinching, / He walked away somewhat, as if he had changed his mind. / Then he caught sight of a cloud of dust; he raised his weapon, / took aim — the dustcloud neared him — but nobody rode up.

X

PROSE TRANSLATION: *A BLESSING. FROM PETRARCH.* Blessed be that year, that month and that week, / and that day, and that portion of the day, and that hour, / and that moment, and that place, where my girl / inspired me with emotions, although she herself does not share them. // Blessed be the shine of those eyes and their gaiety, / [those eyes] from which Cupid peeks out, tensing his little bow, / Blessed be that little *bow, the little arrows and that little boy / who shot at me then, and, ah! shoots at me still. // I bless you, O first untaught song [of mine], / which the forests and rivers of my homeland echoed / and which my fatherland later repeated. // I bless you, O pen, with which long ago / I glorified her, and blessed be my bosom / in which Laura lived, and lives still, for all time.*

— Lines 10-11: In his blessing of that "song" of his, which first echoed about his native places, Mickiewicz uses two geographical terms which are similar enough to be synonyms, and yet slightly different. English does not have exact equivalents for them. First, he speaks of *lasy domowe i rzeki,* which means "the woods and rivers around my house," *domowe* being the adjective formed from *dom* (house), therefore, familiar, native, "homey." Then he speaks of the *ojczysta strona* which repeated the song, later. *Ojczysta* is related to *ojczyzna*, which is Fatherland, i.e. Poland, for Mickiewicz. And thus he seems to be making a suggestion — quite in the spirit of Petrarch — that his first spontaneous song of love in honour of "Laura," which his boyhood region once heard, became famous all throughout Poland, and thus — it is his love for "Laura" upon which his fame as a poet is based. There is an opening outward, from the regional to the national, from the particular to the universal. However (and this is the problem for the scrupulous English translator), Mickiewicz uses *ojczysta* to modify the noun *strona*, which literally means "side," but in a geographical sense, a "region." So *ojczysta strona* might be taken to mean, not the entire nation, but his particular "neck of the woods." This is much less satisfying, as it greatly dilutes the praise of Laura, and the spread of his own fame — and doesn't seem to be much different from those *lasy domowe*. The German translator is in a better position here than his English colleague, for between *Heim* (home) and *Vaterland* (fatherland) he possesses the middle-term *Heimat*, or home region — something with which many Germans identify more closely than they do with the larger German nation as a whole. The same might be true in this case, with Mickiewicz referring here to his *Heimat* of Lithuania, rather than to Poland in general. That such is plausible can be seen from the opening lines of his epic *Pan Tadeusz*, where it is *Litwa* (the Lithuanian provinces of the old Commonwealth) that he identifies as *ojczyzna moja* (my

Fatherland), not *Polska* (or Poland as a whole — which would also have been a perfect metrical fit for the line).

This is another sonnet bearing the subscript "from Petrarch." The Italian model reads as follows:

> *Quando fra l'altre donne ad ora ad ora*
> *Amor vien nel bel viso di costei,*
> *Quanto ciascuna è men bella di lei,*
> *Tanto cresce 'l desio, che m'innamora.*
>
> *I' benedico il loco, e 'l tempo e l'ora,*
> *Che sí alto miraron gli occhi mei.*
>
> *E dico: Anima, assai ringraziar dêi,*
> *Che fosti a tanto onor degnata allora.*
>
> *Da lei ti vien l'amoroso pensero,*
> *Che mentre 'l segui al sommo ben t'invia,*
> *Poco prezzando quel ch'ogni uom desìa;*
>
> *Da lei vien l'animosa leggiadria,*
> *Ch'al ciel ti scorge per destro sentero,*
> *Sí ch'i' vo gir de la speranza altero.*

> Through Laura's eyes Love surveys his empire.
> Laura Love's handmaid, Laura chosen queen.
> So much baser other beauties seem
> Compared to her, so greater my desire.
>
> I bless the hour, the moment, and the place
> My heart first erred in such a lofty zone —
> Thy offering, soul! — Heap up thy hecatombs
> In thanksgiving for such a special grace!
>
> And she transmits that strain of love divine
> Which leads me to the summit of all good
> And teaches me to scorn gross, common vice;

She leads me on to my eternal prize
Encouraging, enlightening the route,
Filling my heart with hope, my eyes with Zion.

XI

PROSE TRANSLATION: *RESIGNATION. Unhappy is he, who vainly calls for reciprocity, / Unhappier is he, whose empty heart afflicts him [with nausea, or boredom], / but in my opinion, he is the unhappiest among all people / who loves no more, but is unable to forget that he once did love. // Seeing flashy eyes and shameless brows, / he poisons the delight that deludes him with memories; / and if grace and virtue will awaken feeling in him, / he does not dare take his overblown heart to the feet of the angel. // He either disdains other people, or he blames himself / he passes by the earthly girl, and steps aside to let the goddess pass, / while, gazing at both, he bids farewell to hope. // And his heart is similar to an ancient temple, / made desolate by foul weather and the passage of ages, / in which divinity does not wish to live, and humans don't dare.*

— Line 8: Mickiewicz uses the adjective *przekwitły*, which connotes a flower gone to seed, overblown, past its prime, faded, no longer of any use or beauty.

XII

PROSE TRANSLATION: *TO***. You look me in the eyes, you sigh; your simplicity is dangerous! / Fear the venom, which burns in the eyes of the viper, / escape, before his poisoned breath overwafts you, / if you don't wish to curse the rest of your life. // One virtue yet remains me: sincerity; / know that it is a base fire that you ignite in my bosom; / but I know how to live a lonely life — so why, with me so near its end, / must an innocent being entangle herself in my fate? // I like luxury, but I'm too proud to seduce; / you are a child, while passionate pain has burnt me through; / you are happy, your place is among happy banqueters, // while mine is amongst the cemeteries and tombs of the past. / Young ivy, wind yourself around a green poplar, / leave it to thorn to wrap around the columns of tombs.*

XIII

PROSE TRANSLATION: *For the first time, I, a slave, am pleased with my slavery: / I look at you, and peace does not disappear from [my] brow; / I think of you, and ease does not disappear from my thoughts; / I love you, and yet my heart does not pain me. // At times in the past I mistook a moment of wantonness for happiness, / at times, my youthful imagination led me madly astray / or a treacherous word, graceful beauty, / but even at such times I cursed my delightful fortune. // Even when I loved her, her, that gift of heaven, / how many tears, what fervour, at times, what dread [there was] / and sorrow now, at the very mention of her name. // Only with you [am I] happy, my dear, only with you! / Praise be to God, Who has bestowed such a lover upon me, / and praised be my lover, who teaches me to praise the Lord God.*

— Lines 3, 4: Mickiewicz describes the lover here as a "slave," and some of his word choices cleverly play off this theme. In line two, where he declares that "ease does not disappear from his thoughts," the word he uses for "ease" — *swoboda* — can also mean "freedom." Likewise, in line 4, where he speaks of "wantonness," that word, *swawola*, is constructed from *swoja [swa] wola,* meaning "one's free will."

XIV

PROSE TRANSLATION: *My dear! I sigh, the memory of [your] heavenly caress / is poisoned by moments of horrid meditation. / Ah! perhaps your heart, which suffered so much, / — perhaps — I am afraid to say it, is devastated with bitter remorse. / Dear, how are you to blame, that the darts of your little eyes / are so flaming, that your lips smile so prettily? / You trusted my virtue too much, too much you trusted your own strength, / and the Creator poured into our beings too much fire. // We battled on for many days, many weeks, / young, always lonely, always together as a pair, / and we were worthy of one another for a long time. // Now, ah! I shall go and drench altars with my tears, / I shall not beg forgiveness for my crime, / But [I shall beg] God not to punish me with your remorse.*

— Line 11: *Byliśmy oboje długo siebie godni* has two meanings. 1) We never acted inappropriately one to the other; 2) We were worthy of each other, i.e. we were well matched, we were made for one another.

XV

PROSE TRANSLATION: *GOOD MORNING. Good morning! I hardly dare wake her, O graceful vision! / Her spirit has half flown off into the regions of paradise, / half remaining to vivify her divine countenance / like the sun half in heaven, half in a silver cloud. // Good morning! Now she's sighed, a ray of sunlight has flashed in her eye; / Good morning! Now the light irritates her eyes, / and wanton flies buzzing round her lips annoy her. / Good morning! The sun is at the window, and I am by your side. // I brought you a sweeter morning greeting, but your sleeping graces / deprived me of boldness; let me first learn: / are you rising with a clement heart? with refreshed health? // Good morning! You won't allow me to kiss your hand? / You make me go away, I'm going: here are your dresses, / get dressed and come out quickly — I'll greet you with Good morning.*

XVI

PROSE TRANSLATION: *GOOD NIGHT. Good night! We won't have any more fun today. / Let the angel of sleep wrap you round in his blue wings [OR: May [[your]] angel wrap you round in the blue wings of sleep], / Good night! let your eyes rest now after tears; / Good night, let your heart be nourished with peace. // Good night! from each moment spent in conversation with me / may some quiet and charming sound remain, / let it play in your ear, and when your thoughts fade into darkness, / then let my image give pleasure to your sleeping eyes. // Good night! turn your little eyes toward me, one more time, / let me kiss you upon the cheek. — Good night! — Do you want to clap for your servants? / Let me kiss your breast. — Good night! all buttoned up. // — Good night! Now you've escaped, and you'd like to slam the door. / [I'll say] Good night to you through the keyhole — Alas! locked! / Repeating "Good night," I'd not let you fall asleep.*

This series of three sonnets (XV-XVII) presents in a lighter, joking manner, a theme found by the poet in Petrarch's *La sera desiar, odiar l'aurora:*

> La sera desiar, odiar l'aurora.
> Soglion questi tranquilli e lieti amanti:
> A me doppia la sera e doglia e pianti,
> La mattina è per me piú felice ora,

Ché spesso in un momento apron allora
L'un sole e l'altro, quasi duo levanti;
Di beltate, e di lume sí sembianti,
Ch'anco il ciel de la terra s'innamora:

Come già fece, allor ché primi rami
Verdeggiar, che nel cor radice m'ànno;
Per cui sempre altrui piú che me stesso ami.

Cosí di me due contrarie ore fanno:
E chi m'acqueta, è ben ragion ch'i' brami;
E tema, ed odi' chi m'adduce affanno.

They burn towards dark and loathe the dawning light.
(Those fortunate in love, that is) — I fear
The dusk, which but doubles the tears
And woe I've undergone the previous night.

The morning has for me far greater worth.
For then I see two brilliant suns arise—
So similar their beauty and their light,
The startled heavens worship dazzling earth.

Just as it was when first the laurel tree
Sprung forth from roots embedded in my breast
And caused me love another more than life,

Thus these two times prompt mixed humours in me:
I sigh after the one that brings me rest
And dread the other that renews my strife.

XVII

PROSE TRANSLATION: *GOOD EVENING. Good evening! this is for me the sweetest greeting; / Never, be that before obstacles come between us at night, / or be it when the morning hour calls me forth again, / do I bid farewell, or greet, with such delight, // as at this moment, emboldened* by the evening shades. / And even you, happy to be silent, yet aflame, / when you hear the greeting "good evening," / you speak to me with a more lively eye, a louder sigh. // Let "Good morning" arise to those who live together, / brightening the work which unites their hands; / let "Good night" embrace happy lovers, // when from the goblet of delight they drink a sweetener for their cares; / but to those, who love, but hide their love from others, / let "Good evening" tone down their all too eloquent eyes.

XVIII

PROSE TRANSLATION: *TO D.D. THE VISIT.* I've only just entered, in hopes of exchanging a few words with her alone: / and already the little bell terrifies me, for in comes a lackey / leading a visitor behind him, bringing bows of greeting and conversation. / Hardly has this one passed out the gate, than another enters. // If I could, I'd surround [your] threshold with a wolves' den, / fox traps, sharp bear traps, / and if weapons were not enough, I'd be ready to escape / into the next world, to protect [us] with a Stygian barrier. // O you damned bore! I count the minutes, / like a criminal awaiting his execution: / while you mumble through your report of the meaningless events of yesterday's ball. // Now you've taken your gloves in hand, and you look for your hat; / now I'll take my second wind, my soul will re-enter my body… / O gods! he sits again, and sits there as if nailed to the chair!

XIX

PROSE TRANSLATION: *TO VISITORS.* If you wish to be a polite guest, read this advice of mine: / It's not enough upon entering to report what everyone already knows, / that today they're waltzing here, and dining there, / that grain is cheap, the rain is falling, and that there are riots in Greece. / If you find two persons keeping pleasant company in the salon, / note well if they forestall you with a bow, or with conversation; / if they're sitting far apart from each other; / if everything is in its place, including their clothing. // If the lady is ready to laugh at every single word, / although her lips don't wish to laugh at all; if the young gentlemen at her side / glances around, and keeps pulling out his watch and putting it back again, // and if he has politeness on his lips, and something evil in his eye: / You know how *you should greet them? — "Be well, farewell." / And when should you visit them again? — In a year.*

XX

PROSE TRANSLATION: *FAREWELL. TO D.D. You push me away? Have I already lost your heart? / But I never had it; — are you protecting your virtue? / Yet you cuddle with another one; — Is it that I don't give you gold? / But I never gave it before, yet I possessed you. // And not for free; although I laid no treasures at your feet, / each bought caress cost me dearly, / on the scales of my soul: a peaceful life; / why do you push me away? — I've sought to understand this in vain. // Today I discover a new greediness in your heart: / You wanted poems of praise! the vain smoke of praise! / For this, then, you toy with the happiness and peace of your fellow men? // The Muses can't be bought! I slipped over each rhyme / as I climbed Parnassus to crown you with a laurel wreath, / and this poem too immediately petrified in my hands, as soon as I mentioned your name.* — Line 13: Like Petrarch, Mickiewicz puns, glancing "laurel wreath" (*lauru zawój*) off the name "Laura."

XXI

PROSE TRANSLATION: *DANAIDS. Fair sex! where is the golden age, when, for wildflowers, / for May dresses embroidered with sheaves of wheat, / the little hearts and graces of maidens were purchased; / when doves were sent to one's dear as matchmakers? // Today's times are cheaper, but the prices more dear. She, to whom I give gold, asks for songs; / She, to whom I give my heart, asks for my hand [in marriage]; She, of whom I sang, asks if I'm wealthy. // Danaids! I've thrown into the bottomless depths of your desires / gifts, songs, and a soul melted in tears; / Today, from a generous man I've grown miserly; from a tender man a mocker. // And although a comely face will still beckon me, / although I must still sing of you and bestow [songs? gifts?] upon you, / before I'd have given everything, today, everything — except my heart.*

— The Danaïds were fifty sisters, the daughters of King Danaos, who fled at the prospect of a marriage with their cousins, the fifty sons of King Aigyptos. When their unwanted suitors succeeded in tracking them down, the girls agreed to marry them, but treacherously murdered them all on their wedding night. Only one girl — Hypermnestra — did not kill her spouse, Lynkeus. The legend of the Danaïds forms the basis for one of the earliest Greek tragedies, the *Supplant Maidens* of Aeschylus.

XXII

PROSE TRANSLATION: *EXCUSE. I sang of love's adventures in a crowd of my contemporaries; / some of them praised me, while others whispered: / "That bard only loves, suffers, and laments; / he feels nothing else, or doesn't know how to sing. // Now that he's entering upon more mature years, with an older reason [[more sense, a settled mind]], / why does his heart burn with such a childish little flame? / Is it for this reason that the gods give him a bardic voice, / so that he'd only croon about himself in each poem?" // A magnanimous warning! — so, right away, like the more elevated spirits, / I grasped the lyre of Alcaeus, but in Ursyn's robes [or: in Ursyn's style] / I'd hardly begun playing, when the whole troop of them // scattered, astonished at what they heard. / So I tore away the strings and tossed the deaf and dumb lyre into the Lethe. / The listener gets the bard he deserves.*

— Line 12: A rather uncertain phrasing. It seems to mean that the listeners were not necessarily ravished with what they heard. After all, the message of the sonnet is that, no matter what he should sing, his listeners will never be satisfied. Adam Rżążewski (Aër) tells us that the sonnet "Apologia" was written in answer to the charges of Mickiewicz's university friend Jan Czeczot: "Czeczot remarked that Mickiewicz wasn't living up to the standards of his role as a national bard, but instead was simply whining on about love." p. 62.

— Julian Ursyn Niemcewicz (1758-1841). One of the most important early Polish Romantics. He was a poet, dramatist and novelist; he was a parliamentarian and a soldier, serving Tadeusz Kościuszko as an adjutant and later sharing his general's imprisonment and exile. For quite a while he lived in exile in New Jersey and acquired American citizenship through marriage. However, he returned to spend the last decades of his life in Poland. Mickiewicz is probably referring to the poet's *Śpiewy historyczne* [Historical Songs], a patriotic collection of verse based on Polish legends and great historical figures.

The Crimean Sonnets

MOTTO
Mickiewicz recycles the motto from Goethe's *Westöstlicher Divan* (1819).

Since the days of Adam Mickiewicz, many of the Crimean locales visited by the poet have undergone a name change. Of the more frequently-mentioned in this work, we may note the following: *Baidar* has been changed to *Orlinoye*; *Kozlov* to *Yevpatoria*; *Kikineis* to *Opolznyevoye*; *Akerman* to *Bielgorod Dniestrovskii*. A complete list of the name-changes may be found in Stanisław Makowski's *Świat sonetów krymskich Adama Mickiewicza* [The World of Adam Mickiewicz's *Crimean Sonnets*].

I
PROSE TRANSLATION: *THE AKERMAN STEPPES. I've sailed out onto a [vast] space of dry ocean; / the cart dips into the greenery, and paddles through it like a boat; / amidst the waves of soughing meadows, amidst the deluge of flowers, / I pass by coral reefs of tall weeds and grasses. // Now dusk falls, and there is neither road nor barrow to be seen; / I look up to the heavens, searching for the stars, those guides of boats; / is that a cloud shining afar off? Is the evening star rising there? / That is the River Dniestr shining, and there has arisen the lamp of Akerman. // Let's pause! — How silent it is! — I hear cranes in flight, / which the eye of the falcon could not overtake; / I hear where a butterfly is swaying on a piece of grass // and where a snake touches the herbs with its slippery bosom. / In such a silence! — Curious, I so strain my ear, / that I might hear a voice from Lithuania. — Let's move on, no one calls.*

Akerman — since 1944 Bielgorod Dniestrovskii — is a town lying about 85km (53 miles) south-west of Odessa. Mickiewicz spent some time here in May, 1825. Makowski (p. 27) relates that this sonnet first bore the title *Podróż do Akermanu* ["Voyage to Akerman"]. The site of the town was colonised by Greeks as early as the IVth c. BC under the name Tyros; the name Akerman dates from 1484, when a Turkish fortress was raised here. Akerman entered into the Russian Empire in 1812.

II

PROSE TRANSLATION: *DOLDRUMS. OFF TARKHANKUT PENINSULA. The wind now barely strokes the ribbon of the pavilion; / the playful, sunlit water swells its quiet bosom; / like a young fiancée dreaming of happiness, /it wakes to sigh, and then again falls asleep. // The sails, like standards when war is over, / drowse on the naked masts; the boat, with gentle motion / rocks, as if it were fastened on a chain; / a sailor takes a rest, and a group of travellers bursts out in laughter. // O sea! amongst your gay little creatures / may be found the octopus, who sleeps in the depths, when the sky is overcast, / but during calm weather flails about its long arms. // O thought! In your depths lies the hydra of memory, / who sleeps during bad fortune and passionate storm; / but when the heart is at peace, it sinks its talons in it.*

III

PROSE TRANSLATION: *SAILING. The roar is louder, more thickly the sea bugbears thread the winds; / A sailor has climbed up the cordage, get ready, children! / He climbs up and stretches out, hanging in an invisible net, / like a spider on the lookout for the trembling of the web. // Wind! — wind! — The ship grumbles, tears away from its harness, / tilts and plunges in the foamy gale, / lifts its neck, and now treads the waves and flies through the heavens, / cleaving the clouds with its brow, catching the wind beneath its wings. // And my spirit bobs through the oceanic tumult like the flying mast, / my imagination swells like the unbraided sails. / Spontaneously, I join the gay troop, happily shouting; / I spread wide my arms, and fall full to the deck. / It seems as if my breast urged on her haste: / How light, for me! How invigorating! How pleasant! I know what it is to be a bird.*

— Line 14: The word *lubo* may be the vocative form of *luba*, i.e. "my darling [girl]." As such, the lonely narrator, here, who had been plagued by bitter memories in the earlier doldrums, now forgets his sorrow and bitterness in the rush of the new experience. He cries out, "ah, my love!" as if in his exaltation he were addressing the girl he'd left behind.

IV

PROSE TRANSLATION: *The sails ripped away, the rudder shattered, the bellowing of the waters, the roar of the snowstorm; / the voices of the terrified group, the ominous groans of the pumps, / the last ropes have been torn from the sailors' hands, / the sun sets bloodily, and with it, the last bit of hope. // The gale howls with triumph, and over the wet mountains / that grow in storeys from the oceanic chaos, / the genius of death ascends and enters the ship / like a soldier storming shattered walls.// These here lie about half-dead, that one wrings his hands, / this one falls into his friends' arms, bidding them farewell, / and these say their prayers before death, in order to ward off death. // One traveller was sitting to the side in silence, thinking: "happy he, who has forfeited his strength, / for he either knows how to pray, or has someone to say goodbye to."*

— Line 6. The word "chaos" (*odmęt*) can also mean "vortex, whirlpool."

"The sea which is not known as the 'Hospitable' Sea for nothing, laid out her treasures before [Mickiewicz] from the very start. On the second day out she allowed him to experience a still [...] and not long afterwards gave him one of the most beautiful attempts at stormy weather that may be encountered on the Euxine. During this gale the poet held out on deck, and when the violent crashing of several waves nearly succeeded in sweeping him off the deck, he caused the sailors to bind him to a bench and thus secured, followed the desperate battle of the elements with a sharp eye." Rżążewski, p. 37.

Much of the imagery in this sonnet may be traced to the descriptions of storms at sea found in Ovid's *Tristia*. See I. 2, ff. and XI. 478 ff. Especially:

> *Dat quoque iam saltus intra cava texta carinae*
> *Fluctus: et, ut miles numero praestantior omni,*
> *Quum saepe adsiluit defensae moenibus urbis,*
> *Spe potitur tandem, laudisque accensus amore*
> *Inter mille viros murum tamen occupat unus.*

> Now leaps into the hollow ship's belly
> The wave, and like the bravest of the lot
> Who will often dash up to the struggling walls
> And win out by hope, fired up by love of praise,
> One man defeat[ing] a thousand fierce defenders.

and

> *Non tenet hic lacrimas, stupet hic, vocat ille beatos,*
> *Funera quos maneant, hic votis numen adorat,*
> *Brachiaque ad caelum, quod non videt, irrita tendens*
> *Poscit opem.*
>
> He can't hold back his tears—this one goes numb,
> Another calls upon the gods, while others
> Just wait upon their funeral. Another,
> Hands raised up to the sky he cannot see,
> Adores the gods with vows, promises gifts.
>   (XI: 524-528; XI: 539-542)

V

PROSE TRANSLATION: *A VIEW OF THE MOUNTAINS FROM THE KOZLOV STEPPES. PILGRIM AND MIRZA. PILGRIM: There? Did Allah set up a sea of ice as a wall? / Did He pour a throne for the angels from frozen cloud? / Did Divon raise those walls from a quarter part of the earth / so as to forbid the caravans of the stars ingress from the east? // What a glow on the summit! The inferno of Tsarograd! / When night spread wide her dun hi'lat, did Allah / suspend that lantern among the circuit of the heavens? // MIRZA: There? I was there. Winter sits there. There I saw the beaks of streams / and the throats of rivers drinking from her [Winter's] nest. / I breathed, and snow flew from my mouth; I hastened my steps, // Where eagles know no roads, where the clouds end their travels; / I passed by thunderclaps drowsing in the cradle of the clouds, / until [I reached] there, where there was nothing above my turban but a star. That's Chatyrdah! // PILGRIM: Ah!!*

VI

PROSE TRANSLATION: *BAKCHYSARAI. Still grand, though now empty, the courtyard of the Gireis! / The thresholds and foyers brushed by the foreheads of bashas, / sofas, thrones of power, the retreats of love, / now the locust skips through, and reptiles wind round. // Through varicoloured windows, bindweed (convulvus), / creeping up the deaf walls and vaults, / takes over the work of man in the name of Nature / and writes in the words of Belshazzar "RUIN."// In the centre of the hall [stands] a vessel of carved marble;/ this is the harem fountain. It yet stands whole / and seeping pearly tears, it cries through the wilderness: // "Where are you, O love, power and praise? / You are supposed to last forever. The spring flows on quickly. / O shame! You've passed away, and the spring remains."*

The palace in Bakchysarai was built in the first half of the XVII century by the Crimean Khan Megli Girei, who named it Bakchy-Sarai or "The Garden Palace." Makowski (p. 58) tells us that until 1825 the palace was in a state of complete disrepair. Later, however, it was renovated three times, which returned it to its original splendour. Decorative materials were imported from Constantinople, as were the Turkish master builders, who installed them. During his stay in Bakchysarai, Mickiewicz took advantage of the free lodging for foreigners provided at the palace. As he wrote in a letter to Joachim Lelewel: "Spałem na sofach Girajów i w laurowym gaiku w szachy grałem z klucznikiem nieboszczyka chana." ["I slept on the sofas of the Gireis and played chess with the late khan's gatekeeper in a laurel-hung verandah" (Makowski, p. 61).

"The description of the fountain belonging to the 'harem' is an invention of the poet's — an attempt at adding a bit more oriental colour to the sonnet. What the inscription actually says is 'Glory to God the Highest! The face of Bakchysarai once more delights in the benevolent care of the enlightened Crimean Khan Girei. He, with liberal hand, hath slaked the thirst of his nation, and as God chooses to help him, will shower on his people still more good works. His swift intelligence hath searched out this famous spring and decreed this splendid fountain to be erected. If there exists anywhere else a similar fountain, let it show itself! We have seen the town of Sham (Damascus), as well as that of Baghdad, yet never have we come across so beautiful a waterspout. The executor of this inscription is named Sheyki. To whomever is thirsty, let the spring itself, by a stream of water spouting from an opening thinner than a finger, say: Come and drink this exceptional water of the clearest spring — *it gives health.'* These last words also signify the year 1176 of the Hajj, i.e. 1762 AD." (Makowski, pp. 69-70).

VII

PROSE TRANSLATION: *BAKCHYSARAI AT NIGHT. The pious locals disperse from the jammids, / the echo of the izan dies away in the quiet evening, / the bashful dusk blushes with ruby-coloured cheek; / the silver king of night hastens to rest beside his lover. // In the harem of the skies sparkle the eternal cressets of the stars / and among them, over the sapphire spaces there sails / one cloud, like a drowsy swan on a lake, / its breast is white, and its edges are painted with gold. // Here shadows fall from minaret and the crown of the cypress; / further on a ring of giant granite hills grow black / like devils seated at the divan of Eblis // beneath a tent of darkness: from time to time, from their summits / a lightning bolt awakens, and with the haste of a faris / flies through the silent desert of blue.*

VIII

PROSE TRANSLATION: *POTOCKA'S TOMB. In the land of spring, amongst delightful orchards, / you withered, young rose! For the moments of the past, / flying away from you like golden butterflies, / cast into the depths of your heart the larvae [insects] of memory. // There in the North, toward Poland, shine groups of stars; / why do so many of them sparkle along that road? / Is it that your eyes, full of fire, before they were extinguished in the grave, / burnt there bright traces, as they so often flew thither? // Polish woman, I too will end my days in lonely mourning; / may some friendly hand toss me a handful of dust here too. / Travellers often converse near your grave, / so the sounds of my native speech would refresh me then, as well. / And the bard, intoning a lonely song about you, / will see a nearby mound and sing for me as well.*

"Above the entryway, situated on the southern side of the mausoleum, an Arabic inscription may be found engraved on a marble tablet: 'May God have mercy on Dilara' or 'Say a prayer for Dilara Bekech.' *Dilara Bekech* means 'Beautiful Maiden'" (Makowski, p. 77). This same author writes of the two legends concerning "Dilara." One version (popularised by Pushkin and Mickiewicz) has it that the girl buried in the tomb is Polish, of the Potocki family; the other holds that the tomb houses a Georgian girl named Mayuma, Zerfi, or Zulinia. Makowski continues: "The beautiful, proud Pole, like her alter-ego, the Georgian, despised the great love of the Khan, who, in the end, decided to free her and send her back to her native land. Moved by the generous intentions of the Khan, Maria at last fell in love with him and became his beloved wife. Shortly thereafter, however, she died. According to some versions of the legend, she was poisoned by a rival… The poet's explanation that a Potocka might have found herself in the Khan's harem as a result of 'the latest Cossack disturbances in the Ukraine' is an historical misunderstanding. Dilara died in 1760. These uprisings, however, broke out in the year 1768. The Polishness of Dilara must therefore remain only a beautiful legend." (pp.77; 78-79; 80; 83).

IX

PROSE TRANSLATION: *HAREM GRAVES. MIRZA, TO PILGRIM: Here, unripe grapes from the vineyard of love / Were taken for Allah's table; here pearls of the East, / from the sea of delight and happiness, were stolen young / by the tomb, the conch of eternity, caught to its gloomy breast. // The curtain of oblivion and time has covered them over; / above them a cold turban shines amidst the garden, / like the bunchuk of an army of shadows; and just barely at its base / their names have been engraved by the hand of the giaour. // O you, roses of Eden! On the slopes of purity / your days bloomed beneath the leaves of modesty, / hidden forever from the eye of the unfaithful. // Now your grave is stained by the gaze of a foreigner, / I allow him to gaze here — Forgive me, great Prophet! / he alone amongst the foreigners has looked on in tears.*

— Line 7. *Bunczuk:* a ball made of horse's hair, used as a standard-ornament among the Turks.

X

PROSE TRANSLATION: *BAIDARY. I set the horse free to the wind, not sparing the lash; / forests, valleys, boulders, one after the other, in a crowd, / flow by my feet and are lost like the waves of a stream; / I wish to inebriate myself, to get drunk on this whirl of images. // And when the foaming stallion no longer heeds my commands, / when the world loses its colours beneath the shroud of the night, / [dream-] images of forests and valleys and boulders / pass reflected in my burning eye as if in a broken mirror. // The earth sleeps, but I cannot; I leap into the bosom of the sea / [as] a black, full swell crashes to the shore, / I bend my forehead in its direction, stretch out my arms, / the wave breaks over my head and chaos surrounds me; / I wait until thought, like a boat spun by a whirlpool, / wanders from its course and is engulfed for a while in oblivion.*

XI

PROSE TRANSLATION: *ALUSHTA BY DAYLIGHT. Already the mountain shrugs its misty hi'lat from its shoulders; / the golden stalks of wheat, ready for harvest, hum with the morning namaz; / the forest bows and spills from its maytime hair / mulberries and pomagranates, as if from a caliph's rosary. // The meadow is in flowers, and above the meadow there are flying flowers, / varicoloured butterflies, like a rainbow's scythe; / further, a locust drags its winged shroud. // And there, where the bald cliff gazes at its reflection in the water, / the sea seethes and rushes with renewed attack, / in its roar[ing swells] light plays as if in a tiger's eyes, // foretelling an even more severe storm for the edge of the world, / while on the depths a billow lightly rocks / with fleets and herds of swans bathing thereon.*

— Lines 3-4: *Like from a caliph's rosary, mulberries and pomegranates.* (The comparison is all the more satisfying in Polish, as the words signifying the fruit (*rubin, granaty*) are also used to describe gems: ruby; garnet, melanite, pyrope).

XII

PROSE TRANSLATION: *ALUSHTA AT NIGHT. The winds become brisker; the daily dryness lessen; / the lamp of the worlds falls upon the* shoulders of Chatyrdah / shatters, and spills out a stream of scarlets / and is extinguished. The errant pilgrim looks around him, and listens: // the mountains have already turned black, in the valleys there is deaf night; / the springs mutter in their sleep on a bed of cornflowers; / the air breathes perfumes, that music of flowers, / and speaks to the heart with a voice mysterious to the ear. // I fall asleep beneath the wings of silence and darkness; / then the blazing sparkle of a meteor wakes me, / heaven and earth and mountains are bathed in a golden flood! // O eastern night! Like an oriental odalisque / you soothe to sleep with caresses, and then, when sleep is close / with the spark of your eye you wake one for further caresses.

XIII

PROSE TRANSLATION: *CHATYRDAH. MIRZA:* Trembling, the Muslim kisses the feet of your rock / O mast of the Crimean ship, great Chatyrdah! / O minaret of the world! O padishah of mountains! / You, above the level of cliffs escaping into the clouds, / sit down at the gate of heaven, like tall / Gabriel guarding the dome of Eden. / The dark forest is your cloak, and janissaries of fear / embroider your turban of clouds with streams of lightning. // Whether we are scorched by sun or shaded in fog, / whether the locust cuts down the harvest or the giaour burns our homes — / O Chatyrdah, you are always deaf and immobile, // between the world and heaven like the drogman of creation / with lands and people and thunderclaps spread beneath your feet, / you listen only to that, what God says to nature.

XIV

PROSE TRANSLATION: *PILGRIM.* At my feet is a land of abundance and beauty, / above my head is the clear sky, and next to me beautiful faces; / why does my heart race away from here to places / afar, and — alas! to even more distant times? // Lithuania! your soughing forests sang more gracefully to me / than the nightingales of Baidar and the maidens of Salhir; / and more gaily did I tread your bogs / than ruby-coloured mulberries, and golden pineapples. // So distant! and such a different enticement attracts me! / Why do I sigh without ceasing, distracted, / for her, whom I loved in the early morning of my days? // She, in that beloved region, of which I was deprived, / where everything speaks to her of a faithful lover — treading in my fresh traces, does she remember me?

— Line 6: In the manuscript version of this sonnet (originally titled *Sonet. W Krymie na Tchatyrdahu*. ["Sonnet. In the Crimea on Tchatyrdah"], line six reads *Niż słowiki wśród laurów, pośród skał krynice* ("Than nightingales among laurels and cliff-springs").

—Line 12. Both *ona* [she] and *dziedzina* [area, region] are grammatically feminine in Polish. Thus, there is some ambiguity to the original. Is the speaker mourning the "region" from which he was forcibly removed, or the woman left behind there?

XV

PROSE TRANSLATION: *PATH AT THE RIM OF THE CHASM IN CHUFUT-KALE. MIRZA AND PILGRIM. MIRZA: Say a prayer, drop the reins, turn aside your face, / here the rider entrusts his reason to the hooves of his horse; / Brave horse! look how he stands, measures the depth with his eye, / kneels, and grips the edge of the cliff with his hoof, // and hangs there. — Don't look that way! There, should the pupil of your eye fall, / as at the Al-Kair well, it will not hit the bottom. / And don't point with your hand — you have no feathers on your arms; / and don't send your thoughts there, because thought, like the anchor // of a small boat tossed into the immeasurable depths / will fall like a lightning bolt; nor will it bite into the seafloor / but will carry the boat along with it into the depths of chaos. // PILGRIM: Mirza, but I looked there! Through the cracks of the world / I saw — what I saw, I will say — [but only] after death, / for there are no words for it in the language of the living.*

— Line 2: The literal meaning of the line, "the rider entrusts his reason to the hooves of his horse," though a little oddly phrased, possesses an intriguing tang. How can you "entrust your reason" to something? Perhaps Mickiewicz was aiming at just such a convoluted expression, in order to reproduce the awesome confusion of the moment. It might be paraphrased as "Here the rider places more trust in his horse's surefootedness than in his own reason, his guiding hand."

— Line 3: In Mickiewicz's day, the word *wiszar* (with its root *wisieć*, i.e. "to hang") was used in reference to any cliff. Today, it has the more specific meaning of clumps of vegetation growing from a cliffside.

XVI

PROSE TRANSLATION: *THE MOUNTAIN KIKINEIS. MIRZA: Look down into the depths — those heavens lying below / is the sea;— it seems that amongst the waves, a bird-mountain, / shot through with a lightning bolt, has stretched out his mast-like feathers / in a ring broader than the half-circle of the rainbow // and has covered the azure fields of the waters with an island of snow. / That island sailing in the depths — that's a cloud! / Her bosom covers half the world in gloomy night. / Can you see the fiery ribbon on her brow? // That is a lightning bolt! — But let us halt, with the chasm at our feet, / we must overleap the gorge at full gallop; / I will jump [first], you be ready with crop and spur. // when I disappear from your eyes, look over at the edge of those cliffs: / If you see a feather shine out there, that will be my cap; / if you don't, no one else should ever come this way.*

"Mickiewicz related the following adventure to his son, which he had experienced in the mountain-pass known as 'Devil's Ladder:'
'I once rode through a tight pass in the mountains with several Russians. On one side of us a high cliff climbed up into the heavens; on the other side lay the abyss. All of us were on horseback and the way was so narrow that it didn't allow for two people to ride abreast. Before me rode a certain Russian, whose horse slipped on the path and plunged down the cliff with its rider from a height of about fifteen feet. I reined in my horse and halted, but my comrades, ignorant of the situation and becoming a bit restless, called to me to move on ahead. To remain much longer in such a place would be to take an unnecessary risk, and, as our guide, a Tatar, pledged to return in search of the unfortunate fellow, we set out again and after a few minutes had left the dangerous pass behind us. We descended into the depths of the valley and after a few hours' ride on horseback found ourselves at a Tatar hamlet.
'Four or five Tatars set out immediately with long rails and ropes in search of our companion. They returned before sunset bearing the

poor fellow on the rails: his horse had been killed on the spot, and he himself was in a frightful state.'" (Quoted by Makowski, pp. 145-46)

— Line 14. Literally: "it is not for people to ride along this road."

XVII

PROSE TRANSLATION: *RUINS OF THE CASTLE IN BALAKLAVA. These castles, broken in orderless ruins, / adorned and protected you, ungrateful Crimea! / Today they jut upwards from the mountains like giant skulls / in which the reptile, or the man baser than a reptile, lives. // Let us climb up the little turret. I seek the traces of a coat of arms; / it is here, as well as an inscription. Here, perhaps, the name of a hero, / who was the terror of armies, now slumbers in oblivion, / wrapped round like a worm in grape leaves. // Here the Greek chiselled Athenian ornamentation on the walls; / From here the Italian fired iron at the Mongols / and the Meccan arrival intoned the namaz. // Today with black wings the vultures wheel around the graves, / as in a city, completely massacred by a plague, / where the black flags of mourning flutter eternally from its bastions.*

XVIII

PROSE TRANSLATION: *AJUDAH. I like to gaze, resting on the cliffs of Judah, / at the foaming billows as, now in black ranks, / compressed, they burst [against the rocks], now like silver snows / they wheel about splendidly in millions of rainbows. // They fret against the shallows, they break into waves, / like an army of whales filling the shore, / conquering the land in triumph, and retreating again, / scattering behind themselves mussels, pearls and coral. // This is like your heart, O young poet! / Passion often brews up dangerous bad weather, / but when you take up your lute, [that passion] without having harmed you / retreats to sink into oblivion / leaving behind it immortal songs, / from which the ages shall weave an adornment for your brow.*

Uncollected Sonnets

PROSE TRANSLATION: *Laura! do those beautiful summers [or years] of our age / still paint themselves in your memory? / When we were alone, and busied only with each other, / and didn't wish to care for the rest of the world, foreign to us. // The cool pantry, which is wound about with green jasmine, / the stream, which winds about the meadow with pleasant sound; / there often, confessing to one another our reciprocal desires, / we were hidden by the loving cloak of the late night. // And the moon, looking out from under a pale cloud, / shone down upon [your] snowy breasts and golden ring, / adding to your graces a divine charm. // At that time [our] hearts were ravished by sweet delight, / [our] lips met, and eye was lost in eye, / tear in tear, and sigh mixed with sigh!*

First collected as Sonnet I of the erotic cycle of *Sonnets*, as published in the 1838 (Paris) edition of volume III of the poet's works, directly following *Forefathers' Eve*.

— Line 7: The verb *tłumaczyć* means "to translate, to explain," which seems odd in this context. Hence, we use the verb "confess."

PROSE TRANSLATION: *How variously shine the flowers on this meadow! / Some are pompous, in gaudy, jovial arrangements, / others were set by friendship — these have been growing for years; / still others seem to be mournfully [wretchedly] withering on graves, / in which hearts and hopes are buried. / When you stroll through this garden of memories, Madame, / perhaps you sigh over some, and burst out laughing at many others. / You will also catch sight of the narrow corner given to me. / And although you cannot value it equally with the others, / although it seems but a lonely little path, / which, because of long suns and intemperate weather, / cannot blossom or green over: / You will yet remember that little path, if even only for this reason, / that it divides the quarters of [your] beautiful garden.*

— "Scrapbook." An *Immionik* is a type of album, in which friends and acquaintances were invited to inscribe a few words. It derives from the word *imię*, that is, first or Christian name — as those who made an inscription would sign their name beneath it. It may also derive from the custom of celebrating one's name day (*imieniny*), on which day invited guests would sign the book as a memento.

— "M.S." Maria Szymanowska (1789 – 1831), Polish concert pianist, and the mother of Celia Szymanowska (1812 – 1855), whom Mickiewicz was to marry in 1834.

— Originally published in the annual *Birut* of 1838, and subsequently included in the poet's *Works* by Józef Tretiak. Writing in Vol. 1 of his *Adam Mickiewicz: Zarys biograficzno-literacki* [Adam Mickiewicz: A Biographical-Literary Sketch], Piotr Chmielowski takes exception to the dating of the sonnet: "Because Mickiewicz's presence in Kowno in August of that year is quite doubtful, perhaps it is necessary to correct the date to "1824 Oct. 26," that is, the day of Mickiewicz's arrival in Kowno," p. 281.
— Line 2: *Szumne*. This word means "gaudy, extravagant," but it also has at its base the word *szum*, meaning a sound like a hum or a sigh — evocative in the context of flowers in a field.

PROSE TRANSLATION: *THE FLEA AND THE RABBI. A certain rabbi, immersed up to his ears in the Talmud, / was suffering on account of a pesky flea: at last, annoyed, / he waited for his chance, and fished him out. [The flea] sat there, fixed [under the rabbi's thumb], wriggling, stretching out his little head and legs. / [He said]: "Forgive me, Rabbi! It's not fitting for a wise man to get angry: / is it proper for a descendant of the Levites to spill blood?" / "Blood for blood!" the Rabbi snarled, "you whelp of Belial! / You Philistine, fattening yourself on another's misfortune! / Ants have their pantry; the diligent swarms [of bees] bring forth honeys and waxes, while drones, drinks: / you alone nourish yourself on blood, / a drunkard all the more harmful, in that it's the blood of others you suck." / He finished, and while he was crushing his prisoner without mercy, / with its dying breath, the flea squeaked, "And how do you make your living, rabbi?"*

— First published in volume I of the 1887 (Leipzig) edition of the poet's *Writings*. In a note to the section entitled "Powiastki i bajki" ["Stories and Fables,"] an editor identifying himself as "P.W." notes that most of these fables, including "The Flea and the Rabbi," were collected from

Mickiewicz's unpublished papers left behind at his death, and from "the album of Mr Piotr Moszyński."

Though it is a fable, we include it here since it has some of the markings of a sonnet: fourteen lines, and the classical thirteen-syllable line characterising much traditional Polish verse, although the rhyme scheme of the original is grounded in couplets.

Quite politically incorrect in our twenty-first century, and — unfortunately — sometimes made use of in anti-Semitic circles on the Internet, the poem must be understood as a joke, and we must beware of applying our sentiments in reference to it, in an anachronistic manner. It must be remembered that Mickiewicz himself was no anti-Semite. Indeed, he himself referred to his own partially Jewish background with pride.

PROSE TRANSLATION: *TO THE SISTER OF MY [FEMALE] FRIEND, WHOM I DO NOT KNOW* [or: *TO THE SISTER OF MY FRIEND, WHOM I HAVE NOT MET / WHO HAS NOT BEEN INTRODUCED TO ME*] *Friends, separated by the sad verdict [of destiny] / when everything on earth places obstacles between them, / select from among the light-rays of the heavens / a star in common, as the witness to their eternal amity. / And by that star, as by the cross, a blessed ring, / they vow, at least, to remember one another. // But there is a more pleasant star, which awakens friendship / in the hearts of two unknown people, parted by distance; / as long as it will shine in the northern sky, / by gazing at it, our eyes at least partially meet. // And when it departs from us, to shine for you / I shall send my gaze, and my wishes, to you along with it. // O! if only more merciful verdicts [of destiny] should allow / [us] to behold that star together, and from near, and for always!*

— Line 4: *powiernica* means "a representative, an agent." We translate it as "witness," because the word is based upon the verb *powierzyć*, meaning "to entrust." However, it also contains the subtle sense of someone being a "go-between" — like a matchmaker, which fits the erotic mood of the poem.

PROSE TRANSLATION: *We parted last night happy and healthy; / last night you became mine — today, with new haste, / with new fire in my eyes and with a bigger [literally: more elevated] smile / I ran up for my happiness, which will be renewed today. // You sigh? You don't wish to show your eyes to your lover? / And my bosom echoes involuntarily / this voice of innocence, frightened by sin, / and my eye too must do homage to shame. // This sadness, this modesty is a new ornament for you. / But if beneath it hide scruples / And it [sadness] would like to gloomily cover over our short joy with an eternal mourning // O lover, the sight of it tears my heart. / I don't want any more of these your sighs and blushes. / Be less perfect to me, and happier.*

PROSE TRANSLATION: *In that spot where, before, lit up by your eyes, / flowers burst forth worthy the brows of an archangel, / later, I plucked you a bouquet from this same meadow, / mixed with wormwood and with weeping willow. // Since weed and fool's parsley will always overshadow [the meadow], / no pure bloom on it will ever take fire; / Even so accept the bouquet: it is not worthy your hand, / yet it grew from earth that had been blessed by your presence. // Ah! my heart is similar to that region: / once near your bosom, in the glorious beauty of youth / it bore for you beautiful emotions and noble deeds. / Today it is maleficent, rank by its own fault, / although for others it suffered long in an insane illness. / Do not disdain it! It was once dedicated to you.*

PROSE TRANSLATION: *THE HAWK. ON THE LATITUDE OF KIKINEIS (TO *). A poor hawk, torn into the wide heavens by a cloud, / which bore him into a foreign element, a distant land, / soaked through by the dew of the seas, exhausted by the gales, / he spreads wide his wings on this mast, amongst people. // But no impious hand shall seize him; / he is as safe as if he were sitting on a forest branch. / He is a guest, Giovanna; he who imprisons a guest, / if he be on the sea, let him fear a storm. // Think on my history, think on your own; / you too, on the ocean of life, saw bugbears, / and I too have been tossed by the wind, my wings soaked through by the spray. // Wherefore then these pleasant words, these treacherous hopes? / Yourself in danger — you set traps for others. [...]*

PROSE TRANSLATION: *Poetry! Where is the wondrous brush in your hand? / When I want to paint, for what reason do thoughts and inspirations / peek from the words, as if through prison bars, / hiding and making foul such poor graces? // Poetry! Where are your melodic sounds? / I sing — but she will not hear my crooning: / just like the nightingale, that king of song, hears not the stream / which sounds its moans in underground depths. // Not only sound and colour, the angels of thought, / but the pen itself, the poet's hardworking slave / does not recognise the rights of its old master on foreign [soil] // and, instead of song, traces incomprehensible symbols: / musical signs of song … but that song, unfortunately, / [will never be sung by her pretty voice].*

PROSE TRANSLATION: *TO SOLITUDE. Solitude! I run to you as if to water / from the quotidian scorching of life; / with what delight do I fall into the bright, pure coolness / of your unsounded crystal depths. // I submerge myself and surface again in thoughts upon thoughts; / I play with them as if they were waves; / until, cooled, exhausted, I lay down my body — / at least for a while — in deep sleep. // You are my element: ah, why is it that your panes of bright waters / cool my heart; shade my sense in darkness, / and why must I again, like a flying fish, / tear myself into the air, in search of the sun with my eye? // And breathless aloft, cold down below, / I am equally in exile in both elements!*

Another untypical "sonnet" of fourteen lines, but with three quatrains (ABAB) and a concluding couplet. As such, it mirrors the Shakespearean sonnet — although the even lines of the quatrains are of eight, rather than thirteen, syllables.

— Line 1: *Samotność* can also be translated as "loneliness."

— Line 7: What we translate as "body" is actually a very strong word in Polish; *zwłoki* is usually employed to signify a corpse.

BIBLIOGRAPHY

PRIMARY SOURCE

MICKIEWICZ, Adam. *Dzieła poetyckie,* ed. Stanisław Pigoń. Warszawa: Cyztelnik, 1983.

MICKIEWICZ, Adam. *Sonety. Podobizna pierwodruku w 150 rocznicę.* Wrocław: Ossolineum, 1976.

SECONDARY SOURCES

JASTRUN, Mieczysław, *Szkic o Adamie Mickiewiczu.* Warszawa: Wydawnictwo "Polonia," 1956.

KUZIAK, Michał. *Inny Mickiewicz.* Gdańsk: Słowo/Obraz terytoria, 2013.

MAKOWSKI, Stanisław. *Świat sonetów krymskich Adama Mickiewicza.* Warszawa: Czytelnik, 1969.

MIŁOSZ, Czesław. *The History of Polish Literature.* Berkeley: University of California Press, 1983.

PETRARCA, Francesco. *Canzoniere,* ed. Marco Santagata. Milano: Arnoldo Mondadori, 2011.

RŻĄŻEWSKI, Adam. *Mickiewicz w Odessie i twórczość jego z tego czasu.* Warszawa: J. Sikorski, 1898.

STEINER, George *The Penguin Book of Modern Verse Translation.* Middlesex: Penguin, 1966.

TARNOWSKI, Stanisław. *Historya literatury polskiej*, Vol. IV: Wiek XIX: 1800-1830. Kraków: Spółka wydawnicza polska w Krakowie, 1904.

WALC, Jan. *Architekt Arki.* Chotomów: Verba, 1991.

WITKOWSKA, Alina. *Literatura romantyzmu.* Warszawa: Państwowy Instytut Wydawniczy, 1987.

ABOUT THE AUTHOR

Adam Mickiewicz (1798–1855) is the national poet of Poland. He was successful in every genre at which he tried his hand, setting the benchmark for excellence in poetry, prose and drama, for all the writers that came after him. His lyric poems, collected in *Ballads and Romances* (1822), ushered in the Romantic Movement in Polish literature. His narrative poems, *Grażyna* (1823) and *Konrad Wallenrod* (1828), reveal his sustained mastery of longer poetic genres. Mickiewicz's epic in twelve books, *Pan Tadeusz* (1834), is universally recognised as Poland's national epic, as well as the last Vergilian epic composed in Europe. *Forefathers' Eve* (available in English translation from Glagoslav) is a four-part monumental drama that deals both with particular themes of Poland's subjugation to the empires of Russia, Prussia and Austria, and general themes — the sense of love, both erotic and Platonic, time and eternity, fellowship and the Communion of the Saints. Compared to the work of Dante and Goethe, it is this masterpiece of Polish monumental drama that elevates Mickiewicz to the ranks of what Eliot liked to call the "great Europeans." The *Erotic* and *Crimean Sonnets* were composed by Mickiewicz in Russia, and on the Crimean Peninsula, in the mid twenties of the nineteenth century, after having been sentenced to interior exile from the Polish and Lithuanian provinces for his supposed insurrectionary leanings. They constitute one of the greatest cycles of sonneteering since Petrarch. The descriptive *Crimean Sonnets* have especially been singled out for their excellence. Among Mickiewicz's prose works, his lectures at the Collège de France on Slavic Literature are noteworthy. Like Byron, to whom he is sometimes compared, Adam Mickiewicz died in southern Europe while attempting to recruit troops to fight against the Tsarist empire.

ABOUT THE TRANSLATOR

Charles S. Kraszewski (b. 1962) is a poet and translator. He is the author of three volumes of original verse (*Diet of Nails; Beast; Chanameed*). Several of his translations of Polish and Czech literature have been published by Glagoslav, among which may be found Adam Mickiewicz's *Forefathers' Eve* (2016), Stanisław Wyspiański's *Acropolis: the Wawel Plays* (2017) and the *Dramatic Works* of Zygmunt Krasiński (2018). His translations into Polish of the poetry of T.S. Eliot, Robinson Jeffers, and Lawrence Ferlinghetti have appeared in the Wrocław monthly *Odra*. He is a member of the Union of Polish Writers Abroad (London) and of the Association of Polish Writers (Kraków).

Acropolis – The Wawel Plays
by Stanisław Wyspiański

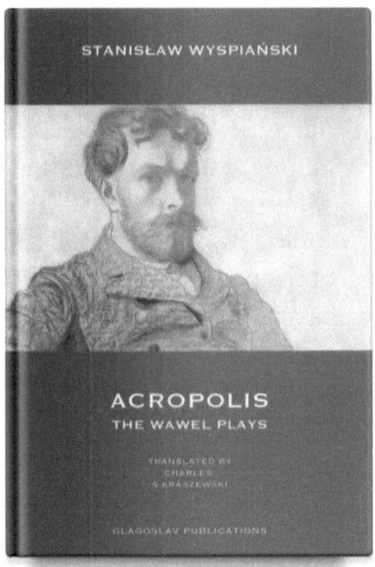

Stanisław Wyspiański (1869-1907) achieved worldwide fame, both as a painter, and Poland's greatest dramatist of the first half of the twentieth century. *Acropolis: the Wawel Plays*, brings together four of Wyspiański's most important dramatic works in a new English translation by Charles S. Kraszewski. All of the plays centre on Wawel Hill: the legendary seat of royal and ecclesiastical power in the poet's native city, the ancient capital of Poland. In these plays, Wyspiański explores the foundational myths of his nation: that of the self-sacrificial Wanda, and the struggle between King Bolesław the Bold and Bishop Stanisław Szczepanowski. In the eponymous play which brings the cycle to an end, Wyspiański carefully considers the value of myth to a nation without political autonomy, soaring in thought into an apocalyptic vision of the future. Richly illustrated with the poet's artwork, *Acropolis: the Wawel Plays* also contains Wyspiański's architectural proposal for the renovation of Wawel Hill, and a detailed critical introduction by the translator. In its plaited presentation of *Bolesław the Bold* and *Skałka*, the translation offers, for the first time, the two plays in the unified, composite format that the poet intended, but was prevented from carrying out by his untimely death.

Buy it > www.glagoslav.com

Forefathers' Eve
by Adam Mickiewicz

Forefathers' Eve [*Dziady*] is a four-part dramatic work begun circa 1820 and completed in 1832 – with Part I published only after the poet's death, in 1860. The drama's title refers to *Dziady*, an ancient Slavic and Lithuanian feast commemorating the dead. This is the grand work of Polish literature, and it is one that elevates Mickiewicz to a position among the "great Europeans" such as Dante and Goethe.

With its Christian background of the Communion of the Saints, revenant spirits, and the interpenetration of the worlds of time and eternity, *Forefathers' Eve* speaks to men and women of all times and places. While it is a truly Polish work – Polish actors covet the role of Gustaw/Konrad in the same way that Anglophone actors covet that of Hamlet – it is one of the most universal works of literature written during the nineteenth century. It has been compared to Goethe's Faust – and rightfully so...

Buy it > www.glagoslav.com

A Brown Man in Russia - Perambulations Through A Siberian Winter
by Vijay Menon

A Brown Man in Russia describes the fantastical travels of a young, colored American traveler as he backpacks across Russia in the middle of winter via the Trans-Siberian. The book is a hybrid between the curmudgeonly travelogues of Paul Theroux and the philosophical works of Robert Pirsig. Styled in the vein of Hofstadter, the author lays out a series of absurd, but true stories followed by a deeper rumination on what they mean and why they matter. Each chapter presents a vivid anecdote from the perspective of the fumbling traveler and concludes with a deeper lesson to be gleaned. For those who recognize the discordant nature of our world in a time ripe for demagoguery and for those who want to make it better, the book is an all too welcome antidote. It explores the current global climate of despair over differences and outputs a very different message – one of hope and shared understanding. At times surreal, at times inappropriate, at times hilarious, and at times deeply human, A Brown Man in Russia is a reminder to those who feel marginalized, hopeless, or endlessly divided that harmony is achievable even in the most unlikely of places.

Buy it > www.glagoslav.com

DEAR READER,

Thank you for purchasing this book.

We at Glagoslav Publications are glad to welcome you, and hope that you find our books to be a source of knowledge and inspiration.

We want to show the beauty and depth of the Slavic region to everyone looking to expand their horizon and learn something new about different cultures, different people, and we believe that with this book we have managed to do just that.

Now that you've got to know us, we want to get to know you. We value communication with our readers and want to hear from you! We offer several options:

– Join our Book Club on Goodreads, Library Thing and Shelfari, and receive special offers and information about our giveaways;

– Share your opinion about our books on Amazon, Barnes & Noble, Waterstones and other bookstores;

– Join us on Facebook and Twitter for updates on our publications and news about our authors;

– Visit our site www.glagoslav.com to check out our Catalogue and subscribe to our Newsletter.

Glagoslav Publications is getting ready to release a new collection and planning some interesting surprises — stay with us to find out!

Glagoslav Publications
Email: contact@glagoslav.com

Glagoslav Publications Catalogue

- *The Time of Women* by Elena Chizhova
- *Andrei Tarkovsky: The Collector of Dreams* by Layla Alexander-Garrett
- *Andrei Tarkovsky - A Life on the Cross* by Lyudmila Boyadzhieva
- *Sin* by Zakhar Prilepin
- *Hardly Ever Otherwise* by Maria Matios
- *Khatyn* by Ales Adamovich
- *The Lost Button* by Irene Rozdobudko
- *Christened with Crosses* by Eduard Kochergin
- *The Vital Needs of the Dead* by Igor Sakhnovsky
- *The Sarabande of Sara's Band* by Larysa Denysenko
- *A Poet and Bin Laden* by Hamid Ismailov
- *Watching The Russians (Dutch Edition)* by Maria Konyukova
- *Kobzar* by Taras Shevchenko
- *The Stone Bridge* by Alexander Terekhov
- *Moryak* by Lee Mandel
- *King Stakh's Wild Hunt* by Uladzimir Karatkevich
- *The Hawks of Peace* by Dmitry Rogozin
- *Harlequin's Costume* by Leonid Yuzefovich
- *Depeche Mode* by Serhii Zhadan
- *The Grand Slam and other stories (Dutch Edition)* by Leonid Andreev
- *METRO 2033 (Dutch Edition)* by Dmitry Glukhovsky
- *METRO 2034 (Dutch Edition)* by Dmitry Glukhovsky
- *A Russian Story* by Eugenia Kononenko
- *Herstories, An Anthology of New Ukrainian Women Prose Writers*
- *The Battle of the Sexes Russian Style* by Nadezhda Ptushkina
- *A Book Without Photographs* by Sergey Shargunov
- *Down Among The Fishes* by Natalka Babina
- *disUNITY* by Anatoly Kudryavitsky
- *Sankya* by Zakhar Prilepin
- *Wolf Messing* by Tatiana Lungin
- *Good Stalin* by Victor Erofeyev

- *Solar Plexus by Rustam Ibragimbekov*
- *Don't Call me a Victim! by Dina Yafasova*
- *Poetin (Dutch Edition) by Chris Hutchins and Alexander Korobko*
- *A History of Belarus by Lubov Bazan*
- *Children's Fashion of the Russian Empire by Alexander Vasiliev*
- *Empire of Corruption - The Russian National Pastime by Vladimir Soloviev*
- *Heroes of the 90s - People and Money. The Modern History of Russian Capitalism*
- *Fifty Highlights from the Russian Literature (Dutch Edition) by Maarten Tengbergen*
- *Bajesvolk (Dutch Edition) by Mikhail Khodorkovsky*
- *Tsarina Alexandra's Diary (Dutch Edition)*
- *Myths about Russia by Vladimir Medinskiy*
- *Boris Yeltsin - The Decade that Shook the World by Boris Minaev*
- *A Man Of Change - A study of the political life of Boris Yeltsin*
- *Sberbank - The Rebirth of Russia's Financial Giant by Evgeny Karasyuk*
- *To Get Ukraine by Oleksandr Shyshko*
- *Asystole by Oleg Pavlov*
- *Gnedich by Maria Rybakova*
- *Marina Tsvetaeva - The Essential Poetry*
- *Multiple Personalities by Tatyana Shcherbina*
- *The Investigator by Margarita Khemlin*
- *The Exile by Zinaida Tulub*
- *Leo Tolstoy – Flight from paradise by Pavel Basinsky*
- *Moscow in the 1930 by Natalia Gromova*
- *Laurus (Dutch edition) by Evgenij Vodolazkin*
- *Prisoner by Anna Nemzer*
- *The Crime of Chernobyl - The Nuclear Goulag by Wladimir Tchertkoff*
- *Alpine Ballad by Vasil Bykau*
- *The Complete Correspondence of Hryhory Skovoroda*

- The Tale of Aypi by Ak Welsapar
- Selected Poems by Lydia Grigorieva
- The Fantastic Worlds of Yuri Vynnychuk
- The Garden of Divine Songs and Collected Poetry of Hryhory Skovoroda
- Adventures in the Slavic Kitchen: A Book of Essays with Recipes
- Seven Signs of the Lion by Michael M. Naydan
- Forefathers' Eve by Adam Mickiewicz
- One-Two by Igor Eliseev
- Girls, be Good by Bojan Babić
- Time of the Octopus by Anatoly Kucherena
- The Grand Harmony by Bohdan Ihor Antonych
- The Selected Lyric Poetry Of Maksym Rylsky
- The Shining Light by Galymkair Mutanov
- The Frontier: 28 Contemporary Ukrainian Poets - An Anthology
- Acropolis - The Wawel Plays by Stanisław Wyspiański
- Contours of the City by Attyla Mohylny
- Conversations Before Silence: The Selected Poetry of Oles Ilchenko
- The Secret History of my Sojourn in Russia by Jaroslav Hašek
- Mirror Sand - An Anthology of Russian Short Poems in English Translation (A Bilingual Edition)
- Maybe We're Leaving by Jan Balaban
- A Brown Man in Russia - Perambulations Through A Siberian Winter by Vijay Menon
- Death of the Snake Catcher by Ak Welsapar
- Hard Times by Ostap Vyshnia
- Nikolai Gumilev's Africa by Nikolai Gumilev
- Vladimir Lenin - How to Become a Leader by Vladlen Loginov
- Soghomon Tehlirian Memories - The Assassination of Talaat
- Duel by Borys Antonenko-Davydovych
- Zinnober's Poppets by Elena Chizhova
- The Hemingway Game by Evgeni Grishkovets
- The Nuremberg Trials by Alexander Zvyagintsev
- Mikhail Bulgakov - The Life and Times by Marietta Chudakova

More coming soon…

www.ingramcontent.com/pod-product-compliance
Lightning Source LLC
Chambersburg PA
CBHW020442110526
44587CB00038B/929